Wilderness Adventures On Horseback
by
Philip J. Beaudet

Forward

These stories are based on fact. Names have been changed to protect the guilty. The horses are themselves because they are. Any resemblance to real or living people or animals is purely in the mind of the dear reader. This book was created for the enjoyment of its readers. Contrary to some who think that there may be a hidden meaning, there is none.

Photographs by Philip Beaudet and/or Pat Horan

Special thanks to my lovely wife, Heidi, and my sister, Judith, for putting up with me.

ISBN: 978-0-6151-4785-7
Copyright © 1994 by Philip J. Beaudet
Wilderness Adventures ©
All Rights Preserved
Printed in Californy

Chapter 1

This was our first year of riding in Yosemite as a team. My partners in this adventurous undertaking were Ron Gabbert and Pat Horan from Santa Cruz, California. I have known them for many years as we all learned to ride and explore together in the Santa Cruz Mountains. We were known for our daring adventures by many of the people living there. We were looking for a ride longer and more challenging than we had found in and around Big Basin State Park. We did not realize that our wish for adventure would come true and thoroughly challenge us.

Our first day was spent fighting with my Dodge pickup truck. We left Santa Cruz at seven AM, but we did not arrive at Yosemite until seven PM. We decided to depart from White Wolf Lodge and spend our first night at Harden Lake, a short three miles away. We checked in with the Curry Company's outfitter and guide at the stables at White Wolf. He told us where the good campsites were at Harden Lake. We talked to him regarding the trail conditions. He said all the trails he had been on that season were in good repair. We thanked him and told him that we would check out with him in five days.

It took us until eight talking to him and saddling our three horses. I was riding El Hassani, my twelve year-old chestnut Arabian gelding who loves to travel. Pat was riding his eighteen-year old Morgan mare, Lady; Ron was on his eight-year old flashy Quarter Horse, Foxy Lady. These were all good veteran trail horses. They were excited as we were about this adventure. It was an easy three mile walk and we arrived at our campsite at Harden Lake just as night fell. It was a little difficult setting up our camp in the dark. We quickly ate dinner and shared the bottle of wine Ron brought. We started to check the horses before turning in, when I ripped out the seat of my old, thin jeans. Pat decided that we should burn the pants in ceremonial style. Fortunately for me, Pat brought an extra set of jeans that fit me perfectly. With the ceremony over, we went to bed just as the moon began to rise.

We were up at six, eager to be on the trail. We planned to ride fifteen miles to Pleasant Valley via Pate Valley. The first few miles were very easy on a nice, well-used trail. We then dropped suddenly into the Grand Canyon of the Tuolumne River. This was an extremely sharp drop off the mountain. Switch backs were cut through the granite mountainside following a water course that at times was a waterfall. This was a very steep trail over slabs of slick granite. It was a challenge, even for us. This was exciting. The view over the canyon was beyond description. It took us a little more than three hours to descend to Pate Valley where we would stop to have lunch.

We were so tired after eating lunch that we took a two hour nap and let the horses eat and rest also. After our nap, we headed up the trail to Pleasant Valley. We had a 3500' climb ahead of us before we would descend another 1000' to the valley. The climb seemed to go on forever and we had to rest the horses many times. We wondered how the backpackers could do all this. The higher we got, more of the canyon was opened up for our viewing pleasure. This was great. The trail was rocky but in good repair. At one point, we came to a level spot that had wildflowers as tall as our horses' backs. Another level spot revealed a large fern grotto nestled amongst shady forest cover. After passing through a corridor through a granite mountainette, we abruptly found a large lakelet covered with lily pads. The wilderness was fantastic in its splendor.

After we reached 8000', we then had to descend to the valley below at 7000'. This descent was even trickier than the one before into Pate Valley. Ron had to dismount and lead his horse down most of it. The weather-polished granite was just too slick for his horse. Hassani and Lady were more sure-footed, but even they had a rough descent. Pleasant Valley didn't have a very large meadow, but after we forded the river we found plenty of grass for the horses. We camped upstream next to a wide raging waterfall. There was a deep pool at the base of the falls where Ron went swimming. Camp was perfect with plenty of level ground.

There were two trees twenty feet apart with a metal pipe between them about twenty feet up. This was for bear bagging your supplies. You could see the claw marks up both trees and even the scratches on the pipe. We would take no chances that night. On my third attempt to throw the nylon rope over the pipe, the whole roll of rope slipped out of my hands and landed twenty feet up in the tree branches. Pat and Ron went into hysterical laughter. We had to throw rocks for thirty minutes to dislodge it. Pat then took over bear bag duty. The only thing that bothered us during our stay in this camp was a single deer looking for scraps of food. It proceeded to eat only our plastic scouring pad. We retired at dark, facing another fifteen mile ride tomorrow.

We started off again at nine AM riding to the top of Rancheria Mountain. The trail was again steep as we climbed to 8100'. At one point, we had to go around a large tree that had fallen across the trail. The only way around the tree was through the hole left by its root ball. I dismounted and walked through it. As I was climbing up the other side, I slipped and fell face down in the soft dirt. Hassani continued around me while Foxy almost jumped on top of me as she tried to jump the entire hole. It was a close call, but I made it without any injuries.

We reached the top shortly and in good spirits where we stopped for a short break. We were headed down to Rancheria Creek at 4600', so we had another 3500' descent. This descent was a lot more gradual and on the top of Rancheria Mountain, with plenty of forest cover and soil to walk on. The temperature was in the high seventies and everything was perfect. We began noticing that this trail received little use and there was a lot of deadfall. Frequently a faint trail would go around the deadfall indicating that it had been there for some time. About two PM the sky clouded over and we could hear the sound of distant thunder. We were well prepared for the high Sierra's habitual afternoon thundershowers so this did not even ruffle our feathers. It soon began raining, so we decided to stop for lunch under the generous cover of the trees. The rain stopped after an hour, just as we finished eating.

The trail conditions worsened as we continued our descent. It took us many extra minutes to find our way around nature's obstacles. Soon we could hear the roar of a waterfall which we presumed to be Rancheria Falls. It took us another 45 minutes before we came to them. It was an awesome sight, water raging down the steep gorge to the waterfall below. The bridge across the gorge did not look right from this distance. As we got closer, we could see that it was badly damaged. It was leaning upstream in a precarious position with a sign on the opposite side facing away from us that read:

"BRIDGE OUT"
"TRAIL CLOSED"

Oh really! They tell us after we traversed that last stretch that the trail was closed. It was no wonder the trail's condition was so bad. We dismounted and inspected the bridge further. Two of the support girders were definitely broken; the third was OK. Only one of the heavy support cables was still attached to the rock. We felt that if we walked over the good girder and cable and distributed our weight out we could safely cross it. We hoped we were right. Ron and I crossed without incident, other than the fact that our hearts had speeded up. As Pat crossed, he closed his eyes as his horse veered off to the weak side. We could hear the bridge creak and we could see it begin to sag. His luck held out as he made it across that insane passage without any problem. That was a rush!!

Within a few hundred yards, we came to the trail junction that we wanted. It had posted the warning and the trail sign pointing out Tiltill Valley where we were now headed. We had another 1000' climb to Tiltill. We had to stop frequently to let the horses catch their breath. It seemed to continue without end. Tiltill Valley was a magnificent sight to behold. It was a

large valley with lush pasture and wildflowers galore. We crossed the north end of the valley on a trail that was built up like a bridge with rocks shoring up either side of the trail. This was more than worth the ride.

We set up camp and turned the horses loose to graze. We decided that on next year's ride we would plan to stay in such a beautiful place for several days or more. This year we had to push on to get back before rescue parties would begin looking for us. We vowed here that we would take the time to ride a week or more together every year in some wilderness or park. Pat took out his knife and proceeded to prick his finger so we could write it in blood. Ron and I did the same. This was paradise.

The next morning we had to backtrack down the trail we had climbed the evening before. It was slow going, but the views of Hetch Hetchy in front of us were spectacular. We were to descend to O'Shaughnessy Dam at 3800'. That was another drop of over 3000'. This was a lot more up and down than we had wanted, but it just meant more work for our horses. We dropped down near lake level a mile or so from the dam. We rode below two majestic waterfalls, Wapama and Tueeulala.

It was about this time when we started encountering day hikers visiting the falls. Just before reaching the dam thing, we had to ride through a dimly lit tunnel blasted or cored through solid rock. The dam gave us a display of water power as a jet of water from the power house continuously sprayed an arc of water across the canyon below.

We now had several miles of paved road to ride on before we reached the trail to Smith Meadow. It was a hot, humid day as we climbed 2600' up Smith Mountain to the meadow near the top. This last climb began to have an obvious effect on Foxy. She began to slow down and lag far behind. At one point we had a twenty minute wait while they caught up with us. During our climb, we saw a forest fire spreading across the top of the mountain which was on the other side of Poopenaut Valley below us. We could see the bombers dropping fire retardant chemicals and helicopters dropping water on the flames below. We lost sight of the activity on that mountain as we neared the top of our final climb of the day.

Within a half hour, I was sure that I could smell the smoke. Suddenly, we came upon a firefighter hurriedly filling his backpack sprayer from the creek. He said there were fires throughout this mountain that were touched off by last night's lightning display that apparently we missed. He suggested that we go back because there were fires everywhere ahead of us. We continued on as there was no turning back for this team. After several easy cross-country detours around the raging infernos, we reached beautiful Smith Meadow. There were many perfect campsites to choose from. Smith Creek partially circled the large meadow supplying us with plenty of water. We were again in an idyllic setting as we kicked back and watched the afternoon's storm approach from over White Wolf and Yosemite Valley beyond. The storm clouds never reached us but we could hear the thunder and on occasion see a lightning flash. We found out, after we got home, that this storm killed several hikers scaling Half Dome. They were apparently struck by lightning while tempting fate. We hit the bedrolls at dark after checking out our six mile ride back to our starting point for our last day's ride.

We left early, but soon we encountered an older forest with a tremendous amount of deadfall littering the trail. It took a lot of time to find our way through the mess. After all the impossible spots we went through, we were confident in our ability to traverse just about anything that lay in our way. Next year, while riding on the Pacific Crest Trail in upper Jack Main Canyon here in Yosemite, our ability to traverse anything was to be thoroughly tested.

It took us about two hours to reach Harden Lake where on the opposite shore we had camped earlier in the week. There was a fenced in pasture with a small, open, usable cabin attached. From this point, we had only three miles and a 400' climb to White Wolf Lodge and an ice-cold Coke. Our pace began to pick up as the horses realized this was the way home. The last mile was done in a restrained run. As we approached the lodge, we slowed down to a prance and observed all the water on the ground from last evening's weather display. We had covered the last three miles from Harden Lake in twenty minutes. The Curry Company guide came out to greet us and he said that he was amazed at the great shape our horses were in. The horses were ready for more and could not believe that this was all there was. The guide said he really didn't think that we would make the route we had shown him. He asked us about the trail conditions on Rancheria Mountain,

which he hadn't ridden for seven years. We told him in detail about the conditions and then went to the store only to find it closed until 1:30. We went back to the truck and quickly loaded up the horses and took off for the Coke machines at the entrance station at Crane Flat.

This was a trip we will remember for a long time. Next year, it would be Pat's turn to select the route we would follow. He vowed that it would be easier and we should have more time to relax and fish.

Chapter 2

We had nine days to ride this trip through Yosemite wilderness and through parts of the Emigrant wilderness. This was to be a more leisurely ride than last year's grueling adventure. This year Ron, Pat, and I planned to do more fishing and relaxing. We did not expect the "E" ticket ride, nor did our newest riding adventurer, Greg.

I was to meet them in a small town south of Stockton along US 99 at ten AM on the 20th of July. I arrived at the Burger King in Manteca a few minutes before ten and waited and waited. They arrived about two PM and we were finally off to the Yosemite entrance at Crane Flat, where we would get our wilderness permit. We informed the ranger of our route and our expected date of departure from the park as was required for regulations and safety. We questioned them regarding trail conditions, weather, and the closed bridge at Rancheria Falls we had to cross last year. They all chipped in their two cents worth "trails are fine," "watch out for bears," "the usual high-Sierra weather," and so on. They said that Rancheria Falls bridge had been repaired and that trail was now opened. We did not have time to check that trail, but we had no bear problems; we had four days of sometimes very heavy rain; and we had problems with trail markings and trail obstacles that almost baffled us for a while.

We arrived at our staging area 1/4 mile from O'Shaughnessy Dam about four PM. We were saddled up and ready to explore this new wilderness experience when a park service ranger drove up. He got out of his truck and strode over to us with his revolver slapping his side with every step. He welcomed us to the park and wanted to see our wilderness permit. I took it out of my saddlebags and handed it to him. Pat mentioned to him that I was from up north where I operate "Wilderness Adventures," a small horse packing outfit out of Redding. He immediately began to interrogate Pat, Ron, and then Greg. When he finished with them he started on me. We finally convinced him this was not a business arrangement and we were all riding together for pleasure in the great outdoors. With that government bullshit out of the way, we proceeded to our evening's camp.

We had to climb 3200' to the top of this mountain along a narrow and, at one time, paved road. At the top of the mountain the road went to Miguel Meadows, and the trail went on to Laurel Lake. We wanted to go on to Laurel Lake to establish camp before dark. It was about eight and we had 2.3 miles still to go. We came upon a large meadow and saw two backpackers trying to throw a bear line over a very tall limb. This distracted us all enough that we missed the shorter of two trails leading to the lake. We rode into camp on the north end of the lake just as night was falling. The lake was a beautiful sight to camp by with the full moon to show us the way. We had plenty of short grass and water for the horses.

Camp was set up in the dark after we cared for the horses. We quickly found wood for our fire and began preparing dinner. We had barbecued hamburgers on sourdough bread with French fries. The ice-cold can of Coke was refreshing. With dinner finished, we hung a bear bag because we were still close to all the weekend campers. We joked about the bears and everyone was to go into bear alert for the night.

I was sleeping soundly inside my dome tent when something woke me. What was it? I heard a sound. It sounded like something moving outside my tent. All I was thinking of was bear. I lay there silently for several moments before I decided to cry out. My shouting "Ron, Pat, Greg, or bear" had no effect other than making the hideous sound outside my tent disappear. I found out next morning it was a deer as I examined the tracks and the damage to our saddle strings where the deer had chewed on them for the salt. This gave everyone a good laugh.

We had breakfast after the horses were turned loose to graze. The venison sausage, eggs, and hash browns were delicious. The horses had an hour for breakfast. We planned an easy, short ride for lunch where they could rest and eat for a couple of hours.

The trail began nice and easy. Everyone commented on the beautiful and spectacular views. We were to continue this fairly level course for an hour before we would drop into Jack Main Canyon. We had expected a moderate descent, but it was very steep with very sharp switch-backs. This is where our "E" ride was to begin. It could be best compared to the Wild Mouse ride found at carnivals. One switchback was so sharp, with huge granite boulders on our uphill side, our horses' heads had to go out over the precipitous ledge before they could swing back to the other direction. This was "a piece of cake" to us veterans of the trail. We made it without mishap and in good spirits. It was about eleven, and we had only about 2.5 miles left to go before lunch.

We found a pleasant campsite by noon. We were next to a large, deep river that had swelled into a small lake with sandy beaches. Pat had become ill from altitude sickness and eating too much breakfast. He turned green, then gray, as he sat next to the tree. Ron and I decided to take a frozen Coke and Ron's TV auction, telescoping fishing pole with reel and go upstream to fish. Actually, Ron wanted to fish; I wanted to sunbathe and watch Ron attempt to catch some fish. It was in the low eighties and the weather was perfect.

Ron and I walked up the trail a few hundred yards and then back down to the river. We were to follow this river up Jack Main Canyon to Dorothy Lake at 9500'. That was to be an easy 1500' climb. Ron spent the next twenty minutes getting his rod and reel ready to go. Within a few minutes, he had caught one of the biggest trout I had ever seen in Yosemite. As he reeled it in, his fishing pole broke in two which allowed that enormous fish to escape. It was a very funny sight. The fish escaped the big white fisherman from Santa Cruz. At least we had the once-frozen Coke to drink.

A large cloud began to cover the sun and it then began to grow chilly. I had enough sunbathing for one day. On the way back to camp, we decided that we would make camp and stay the night here. Pat was setting up his tent when we arrived; he was more than pleased to spend the night. We checked on the horses, then set up our tents to shelter us from the thunderstorm that was brewing. It came and dropped a sprinkling of moisture and was then gone. We then decided it was time for a fire and dinner.

Tonight we would dine on Zorro steaks and potatoes au gratin. We also had sourdough bread and mocha mousse pie with a can of ice-cold Coke for each of us on the side. We were dining by the bank of this swiftly flowing river watching the fish pass us by. The greenery and rock formations before dusk were beyond compare. It was dinner in Paradise. Tomorrow we had only 12 easy miles to reach our camp at Dorothy Lake.

We packed up early and were on the trail by nine. It was going to be another beautiful day. We rode along the river watching the fish swimming and jumping. They were just begging Ron to try again with his crippled, deformed pole. We stopped on numerous occasions to admire and photograph the scenes unfolding before us.

Just before we arrived at Wilmer Lake, we came to a gate in the fencing. It appeared that the trail would pass through the gate and miss the lake but we finally came to the Pacific Crest Trail junction which went back the few hundred yards to the lake. Also, at this trail junction, we spotted the remains of an old cabin and then spotted a man working on its inside. He was the back country ranger and this was what the avalanche did to his post. He needed a crew of three good men for a week to restore the cabin, but the park service sent him in alone because he had carpentry skills and it had no money in the budget. He was very polite and told us about the trail conditions ahead including the avalanche we had to cross. He had made it through with his horse and mule so we would have no trouble at all. We went back to Wilmer Lake as his horse and mule watched. We had a great lunch and rested while the horses drank and ate their fill of water and grass.

We had about nine miles to go which should have taken us about three hours. The first hour was easy going with plenty of grass and the river at our side. We came across a backpacking party of five and stopped to talk with them. They told us of the 1/2 mile long avalanche across the trail ahead of us. It took them three hours to traverse it. We told them that we knew it would be a challenge, but we could do it and then we were off. A surprise awaited the four of us.

We came to the slide area within a half hour. There were downed trees, broken trees, rocks, and even some snow everywhere and trees lying in every conceivable angle. Yes, this was to be a real challenge, but we made it in about a half hour. We continued up the trail happy that it only took us a half hour to cross that mess.

Fifteen minutes further up the trail we found the real avalanche. It was an awe inspiring sight and seemed to continue without any end. We had to get off the horses and leave them behind while we scouted a way through this seemingly impenetrable barrier.

It was extremely rough going up and over and through the downed timber and snow. This was even more tiring at our elevation of 9000'. I had begun to think it looked impossible when I could hear Pat shouting that he had found a way. He did, but it was treacherous, especially while trying to lead two horses at once through the twisted maze of fallen timber. We finally made it with only a few cuts, scrapes and bruises on man and horse alike just as the rain began to fall.

We rode into camp at Dorothy Lake a little wet and cold, so we quickly built a large fire and turned the horses out to graze. The tents were quickly set up and we began to prepare dinner. The wind had picked up and was soon blowing a chilly rain into our camp. The trees soon began to drip on us as well. We continued, dinner which consisted of lobster, potatoes au gratin, and wine. We also consumed nearly a third of Pat's brandy. By dark the rain had stopped, although the cloud cover still looked threatening. We were anticipating more rain during the night. It rained and then rained some more.

Greg woke us all about sunrise with a big roaring fire. He had not slept at all during the night because he was so wet and cold. He hadn't counted on such weather in the middle of summer. We all sat around the fire drying articles of our clothing and eating our breakfast consisting of fresh scrambled eggs and elk sausage. The horses survived the storm while standing tied to a picket line set up in the trees.

We got a late start that morning because of all the things we wanted to dry. On the trail to the camp we had come up on yesterday, we had passed a trail marked Bond Pass, and later another unmarked and faint but obvious trail heading up the same way. Ron and I decided that it was a shortcut to the pass and so led the way up this faint trail. I stopped Ron after a half hour of riding and asked where Pat and Greg had gone. He said that Greg and Pat had hung back to take photographs. We continued climbing toward Bond Pass, expecting them to bring up the rear. The trail began to get gnarly in many spots. The rocks and narrow passages were difficult for the horses to negotiate. Just as we reached the glacier-covered pass, Pat and Greg rode up. Pat was furious with us taking the wrong trail. I pointed out to him that this sign said Bond Pass, so we made it on this "wrong" trail. I am still scratching my head about where the "real" trail is as we never found it at the top. Also, on the Bond Pass sign was another sign indicating that the trail we had just climbed up was

"ROUGH."

Thank you, Park Service personnel, for letting us know after the fact the trail conditions.

We had planned to stay at the top for lunch but another storm was building fast and we did not want to be caught at the top of a 10,000' mountain pass during a thunderstorm. We made tracks down an old jeep trail as we entered the Emigrant Wilderness. The rain was just beginning in earnest as we searched for some shelter. We found a snow survey cabin, but it was locked up with government

"No Trespassing"

signs everywhere. Well, we thought that this summer storm would be over in a few hours at most, so we decided to stick it out and have lunch. Instead of letting up, the storm became much more severe. A light, wet snow began to fall as the temperature took a nose dive. We decided that we should leave the scant shelter of trees and look for a better site for us and for the horses. We rode to Snow Lake and found an old mining relic of a mobile home made of wood and on skids. There was a large fire ring under a very large tree. Greg proceeded to build a bonfire to warm us and the whole neighborhood while we assessed our situation.

We were at 9500' and wanted to be at a lower elevation to try to get out of the most severe part of the storm. The two routes we had planned on following earlier remained at 10,000' for a day or more. We had another alternative on our map that we had not considered, and that was Huckleberry Lake a short nine miles or so away. What we did not know was that the trail went over a glacier on its way to Huckleberry Lake.

We were drying off in front of Greg's barn burner when up walked a backpacker in full regalia. She was on her way to Dorothy Lake when she saw our fire. We asked her to stay and warm up with us by the fire as she told us of the trail conditions she had seen. She said that she had just been over the trail we were planning to take. She pointed out the saddle at 9600' with the glacier flowing through it. We were beginning to wonder about our choice of trails when the heavy rain became worse and then the wet snow began to fall. Since Huckleberry was closest and was a drop to 8000', we decided to try the glacial crossing of that foreboding looking saddle.

The heavy rain turned to a light drizzle as we began saddling up. Our ride to the glacier was done in a light mist that was really pleasant now that we had been warmed by the fire. The brush got our legs and feet wet. The trail was easy to follow until we came upon that large sheet of ice. We could easily follow the backpacker's tracks through the wet snow. The horses didn't hesitate to cross until her tracks made a sharp turn up slope. There was a brief moment of flying hooves as we regained control of our mounts. We proceeded through the snow capped glacier, occasionally up to the horses' knees in snow. As we neared the top, we lost sight of her tracks in the fresh snow and had to proceed blindly over the wind-swept saddle and down the other side. It took us a while to find the trail again after we left the glacier.

The rest of the way the storm continued to drizzle on us. It was no longer as cold as it had been but enough to stiffen all of us. We didn't do too much talking. We finally arrived at Huckleberry Lake about five and turned the horses loose to graze on the lush grass. Our camp was in a large, flat wooded area up against some very large boulders. We quickly set up camp and built another fire to warm up our chilled and stiff bodies.

We were sitting by the fire when a young boy scout appeared from out of the wilderness carrying three large trout which he offered to us. We quickly decided to have buttered fried trout for dinner instead of the steaks we had planned on. There is no way to describe how good that fish tasted that cold dreary evening. The scout had fed the group he was with all the fish they wanted to eat. These were just the culls. He said he caught them at Emigrant Lake earlier in the day. This got Ron all excited and he proceeded to put his fractured pole back together with band-aids. It was dark before he finished, so he decided to spend tomorrow fishing with the two night-crawlers the scout had left him.

The storm worsened during the night and dropped a tremendous amount of rain on us. We stayed warm and dry even with the rain; well, everything but our boots. The morning brought cloudy skies but at least it was not raining. We decided to stay at this camp and weather the storm. Pat, Greg, and I decided to saddle up and explore some old mine relics we had passed yesterday along the side of the trail. We left Ron in camp where he was still trying to get his rod and reel ready to catch the fish of his dreams.

The ride back to the mine was drier than we thought it would be. We spent a few hours looking through the artifacts remaining around the blasted mine shaft. The cloud cover was letting up and we even had a few moments of sunshine. We started back to camp with the warm sun at our backs. Just as we neared camp, the sky burst overhead and it began raining as hard as before. Ron had aborted his fishing to rush back to camp to try to put everything under cover. We all reached camp simultaneously and quickly put things away and took cover, but we still got very wet. We wondered if this was ever going to let up.

After a few hours, the heavy rain let up to a light drizzle. We decided that it was now time for our dinner and we should take advantage of the light drizzle and prepare our food while we still could. Ron's pole had acquired a few new fractures during his attempt at fishing, so he was unable to provide the fish we were expecting. We had three steaks left, so we made a delicious beef Stroganoff with raspberry cobbler for dessert. The sky was clear by dusk and we went to bed under clear skies. We would wait until checking out the morning's weather before making our trail plans for tomorrow or the following days.

The morning brought us sun and not a trace of clouds were to be found. The storm was over and we decided to pack up. We planned to head up and over about seven miles to Cow Meadow Lakes. We started off down the trail and found a lot of deadfall we had to detour around. After the last detour, we lost the trail somehow while trying to negotiate the boulders and brush. Ron wanted to fish some more so we stopped at a pleasant place at the real Huckleberry Lake and fished for a few hours. With Pat's expert advice, Ron finally managed to catch a few good-sized trout, which we put in the ice chest for dinner later that evening.

We had to backtrack to find the trail. That was not an easy task through the thick brush and large boulders. We finally found it and proceeded to ascend this granite mountain populated with a little dirt and even fewer trees. The going was treacherous, to put it mildly. At one point, we were climbing up a V-shaped ledge about 50' long with a 7 - 15' drop to the brush covered boulders below. Ron made it up first to the next level of the ascent. Greg was close behind with the pack horse and I behind him. Greg's horse decided he was not going up and since he couldn't go back down, he took the only reasonable approach left. He jumped. Fortunately, Greg fell clear as his horse performed equine gymnastics for us. Neither received any serious injuries. We made it up that nasty stretch without further incident.

We were still on the trail to Cow Meadow Lakes when Greg's horse lost a shoe. Being a horseshoer by profession, Greg had a relatively easy time replacing the lost shoe. We came again to a nasty spot climbing up a steep piece of trail. It too was a V-shaped ledge with a small drop-off to the right to rocks below. Greg decided it would be safer if he got off and walked his horse up it. While hiking up the rocky trail, his boot got caught between some rocks and he fell in front of his horse scrambling up the trail right behind him. He rolled off the ledge to the rocks below, just missing being struck by his horse's flying hooves. This time Greg sustained a few injuries. He had hurt his arm, and although it was not serious, it was very painful.

This was definitely not an easy trail even for experienced riders such as us. We finally made it to the top where the trail junctioned with the trail back down to the southwest shore of Huckleberry Lake.

The trail we just came up was marked:

"ROUGH TRAIL."

Thank you, Forest Service, for the well-marked and maintained trails.

We now were on a much better trail, although it was still tricky footing sometimes for the horses. It was still a steep and rocky trail to the lake below. Along this trail there appeared a small turquoise, needlelike plant. These "plants" turned out to be nylon bristles attached to nail heads and planted in the ground, sometimes near the trail. What was their purpose? During our descent to the lake, the sky began clouding over again. By the time we reached the lake, it was again raining on us. The lightning was in this basin with us. We reached the river flowing into the Cow Meadow Lake and found a wide sandy spot to ford. The trail across the river went to the right, up to Emigrant Lake. We took the left branch of the trail to go to Cow Meadow lakes and to begin looking for a campsite.

The trail started to climb after we met a couple of backpackers readying themselves to strike camp. I noticed, after 20 minutes of climbing, we were on the wrong trail and were leaving the lake. Greg's horse decided again to lose a shoe, so Greg could practice wilderness horseshoing for a second time. We had just come to a big burning tree that the lightning had struck right on the trail. We quickly turned around and headed back down to the lake, passing the backpackers on their way out. Back at their camp was where we had missed our trail around the lake and down the canyon. It was here we noticed that we only had part of Ron's fishing rod and reel left. The remains were strung out behind us still attached to us by the unwound fishing line. There was no way we were going after it!

We continued to look for a camp along the river/lake (we couldn't decide what it was). We came across one really nice spot, but it wasn't along the lake, so we pushed onward. The trail continued along the river and kept getting closer to it. Without any warning, the trail went into the river where a very large outcropping of granite forced it into the water. Ron's horse gave us a show of jumping off the underwater trail ledge and took Ron swimming. The trail made this river walk a few more times before we finally left the lake and came to nothing but granite.

With the weather getting worse, we turned around and headed back to the campsite we saw earlier. We again went through the river with Ron complaining the whole way. Just as we reached our destination, it began to hail heavily. The hailstones grew larger and larger. We had to take shelter under trees as we watched the ground whiten around us. It stopped after 20 minutes, so we could establish camp in the rain that followed. The rain persisted as a drizzle for the rest of the afternoon.

We soon had our fire going and we were warming ourselves up. The horses were grazing in a large meadow of grass along the river bank. We were still at 8000' but it was not really cold. We had Ron's trout and beef stew for dinner. We had our last Coke Classic and cherry cheesecake for dessert. As we finished the last of our dinner, a man, wife, and their child

went riding by, leading their pack horse. They had just come up the trail from where we were going tomorrow, so we now knew the trail continued past the granite where we lost it earlier. We went to bed under clear skies, expecting an easy 12 mile stretch tomorrow. We had no idea what was in store for us.

It was a beautiful morning without a cloud in the sky. We got an early start, leaving at nine. We all felt good except Ron, who was not going to cross that stretch of trail where he gave us our swimming lesson yesterday afternoon. He soon found out that there was no better way than that, so he crossed without further ado. Once on the massive slab of rock that the trail traversed, we had nothing but ducks (rocks) placed in such a way to be obviously of human placement, marking a trail to show us the way. This would have been challenging enough without the slick rock, cliffs, precipices, gorges, and other treacherous obstacles that defy description. The weather, environment, and lack of maintenance had left us with only a few ducks and, occasionally, conflicting ducks to try to follow. The remaining part of this eight mile stretch of trail had to be found by using all our trail finding and map reading abilities.

Finding the trail on foot wearing hiking boots would be fairly easy, although strenuous. Finding a trail passable for the horses wearing steel shoes was not easy, nor was leading two horses at once across that trail of slippery rock. I found out also that leading a pack horse with an impatient Arab, whose hackamore was put on backwards, was not an easy feat. It is almost impossible to imagine the vastness of granite mountains and gorges ever being traversed by horses. It could be done, but the risk factor was very high. This was definitely an "E" ticket ride.

Several times we were able to find a small forest with dirt to walk on and, at times, tread we could follow. This was not always easy, however. The deadfall was atrocious. Once, while leaving the forest, we had to cross two logs before hitting the granite again. Ron's horse jumped the first; he was off balance for the first jump when his horse jumped the second one. That was enough to send Ron rolling toward the ledge of a 200' drop to the river and rocks below. He stopped face down with his arms outstretched towards the drop below. Ron slowly turned over with his cigar still hanging from his mouth and a wide grin on his face. Then the cussing began. He had hurt his wrist pretty badly, possibly a break. We wrapped it tightly and continued this day's adventure.

Pat was the next to have a major mishap. He was in the lead riding Shab, when on a slicker-than-most section of granite Shab faltered and went down, sliding into and under a massive boulder on his downhill side. Shab was frightened and thrashing wildly to get out from underneath the boulder and get to his feet. In the process, he kept banging his head on the rock above. This left him cut and bruised about the head and on his legs. Pat finally managed to pull his head around and Shab scrambled to his feet. He was shaking with fright with a glazed look in his eyes. After a few minutes of talking gently to him, he was relaxed enough to continue. Pat went uninjured through this traumatic experience with nothing other than a few sore muscles and a racing heart. The rest of us decided to find another route and meet Pat down the "trail."

We continued down this canyon that had so many hazards they defy description. At one point, the tall cliffs on our right started closing in on us and the river below. It looked as though we were coming to a steep, narrow gorge that would not permit us passage. As we got closer, we could see it was a gorge but that there was a crude, horrifying trail blasted out of the granite rock barely wide enough for our horses. We all dismounted and walked along this 100' long, loud, insane passage to a wider part of trail ahead beyond the falls. The horses did very well through all that with no surprises for us at all.

The trail got no better after we passed through the gorge. The map showed us crossing two rivers where Huckleberry Canyon joined ours. It appeared that we may have passed our point of crossing, so we began looking for a place to cross to the peninsula separating the two raging rivers which appeared across from us here. The river was deep but we experienced no problems in crossing.

We wound up on the flat peninsula that was heavily forested and loaded with deadfall. It took some time to traverse this small stretch, but we soon stumbled upon a well-constructed camp next to the other river crossing. There was an abundance of water but no grass for the horses, although the map showed a meadow. We were getting tired and irritable from all the problems this "trail" was causing us as we crossed the river and junctioned with the Huckleberry Lake trail.

Fortunately, this trail was a little better laid out than the one we just left. The trail had portions of its tread blasted out which gave us better footing than the slick granite we just crossed. Things were beginning to look up for us. We were Now riding on massive slabs of granite piled on top of each other looking like sliced, fried potatoes served on a dish, but which had actually fallen in slabs from the mountain to our left. The trail climbed up this mountainside toward Styx Pass, where we would reenter Yosemite National Park. The sky was beginning to cloud up the sky as we climbed toward the pass.

We reached Styx Pass with no further trouble or rain, which thoroughly surprised us all. The trail inside the park was much better even though it was over much of the same terrain. We were all pretty tired from this day's adventure, but we still needed water and grass for the horses. The closest water and possible grass was about three miles down our trail. The trail gradually left the rock as we began to enter more forested lands. We came across a pond with a little grass and thought we had found Swede's camp that was shown on our map.

We could not find a camp, so we carved out our own on the far shore of the pond. The grass was in amongst a lot of brush and the water was drinkable only for the horses. That did not stop us from having a comfortable camp with hamburgers and Mexican casserole for dinner with apple cobbler for dessert. Since we were approaching the civilized area of the park, we decided it was again time to bear bag the food. After several failed attempts at pulling our pack with food up more than six feet, we left it there and went to bed on bear alert. No bears tried to mess with this rough outfit.

The next morning brought us sun and clear skies again. We started out about seven-thirty, so we could get water for us to cook and clean with. After a half mile, we came across an old sign indicating that this was Swede's camp. We missed it. It was of no use to us because it lacked water and grass. The map showed us a spring about 2.5 miles ahead, so that was where we headed. We hadn't found it within an hour but we soon found a nice level area with good grass, so we stopped. We sent Greg down the trail with the canteens for water while we unloaded the horses. We expected him back in a few minutes but it took him almost an hour. Apparently the spring on the map was not correctly marked, so he had to travel quite a bit further than expected. We had stopped right on the trail junction of the Kibbie Lake trail and so could observe the trail's traffic with ease. This Friday afternoon brought many weekend campers heading to the lake for the usual weekend orgy. We sat here for several hours eating, then napping. It was a beautiful day, though quite warm.

We saddled up and proceeded to head down to 3800' and cross the dam across Lake Eleanor. It was a hot and dusty descent. The trail showed no evidence of the storms we had experienced during the last four days. There was proof of people everywhere. We had lost our wilderness experience. We crossed the dam below Lake Eleanor and came to a ranger station where we again met a ranger that placed great importance on our wilderness permit. It was stored with our supplies in the packs on the pack horse, so it was not easy to get out. After a short discussion, he finally agreed to just take down our names and destination. While he was doing so, I told him about the poorly-maintained trails and lack of proper trail markings in the places we had been this year. He said that budget cutbacks allowed him only time to pick up refuse and check for permits. We told him we were on our way to Miguel Meadows to spend the night and then left him with his paperwork.

The trail to Miguel Meadows was the same partially-paved old road we climbed out of Hetch Hetchy eight days earlier. It was a wide trail where we could ride two abreast and talk. It was along this stretch that my horse lost a shoe. He actually was wearing the shoes out even with three points of borium on them. Since it was only six miles or so next day and because he does well without shoes, I did not replace it. At Miguel Meadow we found a ranger station, toilets, campsites, fenced pasture and barn, and tools without rust lying on the cabin's porch. There was no water nor a person to be found. We set up a large camp and proceeded to enjoy our last evening in Yosemite this year. We heated up my famous elk stew and pigged out. We had raspberry and apple cobbler for dessert.

As it started to get dark, Ron went down to check the horses. He came running back shouting that all the horses except Shab and Hassani, who were picketed, had hit the trail without us. Shab was all excited, but Hassani wasn't interested enough to stop eating. I untied him and started looking for the others from his back using nothing but his halter and lead rope. I searched all the close places first but they were not there. I started down the road in the direction we would take in the morning, but turned around when Hassani became too much to handle with just the halter. I ran back to camp and saddled him up and took off just as Pat was rounding the bend leading the horses back. He found them coming back from down the road a few hundred yards past where I had turned around. Another adventure was successfully completed. With the horses tied up for the night on a picket line, we returned to the camp to make more dessert and try to decide how we would bear bag our supplies. We had no food left and no tree to hang it from, so we left it on the ground. Apparently all the bears were with the weekend campers and their easy pickings.

It was a warm night down here at 5200' but it was far cooler than our descent back down into Hetch Hetchy was to be tomorrow. We had an easy ride on the old road for the three miles before we junctioned with the same trail we started nine days before. We had come full circle and passed all the tests nature and civil servants could toss at us, except one. I had lost our wilderness permit somewhere in camp at Miguel Meadows. We hoped we were not going to have to produce it again. As we descended into Hetch Hetchy, the temperature began to climb. Ron's horse nearly stepped on a huge rattlesnake sunning itself on the road before we spotted it and it slithered off the trail. We rode the rest of the way without incident; it was a cake walk.

This was without doubt the most challenging of any wilderness experience I had ever had, some of which I would never want to repeat. It is a difficult and dangerous pursuit taking horses across such terrain, but at the same time you have to admire your ability to do so.

Chapter 3

This year's Yosemite trip was not actually within the confines of the national park, but the wilderness borders the park on its northwest boundary. Pat Horan and Ron Gabbert were again joining me on this Wilderness Adventure. Two old friends, Chuck and Cord Wood, were also riding with us. This year's story must first begin several days before the ride was to commence.

I purchased my first set of EasyBoots on July 23, '87 after reading the brochure titled "Special Tips for Riders" who really use their horses. My horse's hooves were brittle and would not hold a shoe. This was the time to try EasyBoots. I purchased them from a veterinary hospital after discussing the instructions with the veterinary assistant on how to properly apply the Easyboot to the horses hooves. I read the instruction sheet and then underlined all the important points.

I began on the Friday morning before the trip. I trimmed all four feet and put on the left front boot to check the size. The boot fit tightly. The inside strap fit tightly below the hairline and below the heel bulbs. The back of the boot rubbed above the hairline. I removed the boot and cut the back of the boot to avoid any chafing. The metal prongs were then slightly bent toward the hoof to form a downward angle with the hoof as stated in the instruction sheet. I used 1/2 tube of silicone sealer inside the boot. The boot was then applied to the horse's hoof and the cable clamp was tightly fastened. I used my hammer on the sides of the boots where the metal spikes were to drive them down into the hoof. I then followed the same procedure with the other three boots. I now had 24 hours before the ride to allow the silicone seal to set.

The first problem arose as I was unloading my horse from the trailer at the wilderness trail head at Crabtree Camp. The right front boot came off. Upon inspection of the boot, I observed that the cable had broken. It took some time, patience, and a little baling wire to repair the boot.

The second problem occurred as we crossed a shallow, sandy creek. Two boots came off, and a third was lost on the soft dirt on the bank. This was not what I had in mind when I thought of EasyBoots. My friends were in hysterics over my frustrations. They were now calling them "easyoffs". I proceeded to replace the three boots and try them again on the soft terrain we had to travel on now. I again hammered in the spikes and securely fastened the cable clamps to assure a snug fit.

We were off again. I had Pat ride behind me to watch for the loss of a boot. Within 20 minutes, I had again lost two boots. I decided to tie them onto the pack horse. We then began climbing and encountered moderate sized granite rocks on the trail. Within minutes, I had lost another boot. This was enough! Whiskey was just going to have to make this trip barefoot. We continued on our way to Grouse Lake at 7500'.

Camp was established at the east end of the lake. There was sufficient grass, but the horses had to remain picketed due to the proximity of the trail with plenty of traffic. Pat prepared the best tasting and the messiest tacos I have ever eaten. The cherry cheesecake topped off an excellent dinner.

The next morning I broke out the tools and sheet metal screws and began again putting an EasyBoot on each hoof. I then put a sheet metal screw into each side of each boot. I used washers under each screw and screwed the screw into each hoof as stated in the instructions in the Special Tips handout that came with the boots. By now, my friends knew I had really taken leave of my senses.

We set out later than usual because of the EasyBoot installation. We began climbing over huge slabs of granite. I kept watching the boots and riding more carefully than usual. Thirty minutes went by and I was finally beginning to relax. We stopped for a break soon after and I noticed that I was missing two boots. I took off the other two and tied them onto the pack horse. I was piqued, to say the least.

What was wrong with these boots? What was I doing wrong? Is the outdoors too much for them? They surely did not live up to their advertising. I was very disappointed!

We headed out toward Groundhog Meadow. Once there, we turned north onto a light trail that headed to Piute Meadow via Piute Creek. At the meadow, we turned east onto a faint tread through jumbled rocks. Halfway up one particularly difficult stretch, I noticed that we had lost the pair of EasyBoots which had been so securely fastened to the saddlebags with baling wire.

We soon came across little pristine Piute Lake. It was here that I noticed that our pack horse, Chickadee, had a shoe that was ready to come off. We stopped and unpacked the pack horse and the packs to retrieve our tools from the bottom of the panniers. The shoe was easily reset, so we quickly finished repacking. The entire stop took us only 1 1/2 hours. We continued on our way to Buck Lakes where we planned to spend the night. The scenery was terrific and the lack of people was refreshing. The weather was brisk with a slight breeze. We passed Gem and Jewelry Lake, but as we were ready to cross the creek above Deer Lake, we noticed that Shab had now lost a shoe. After another 1 1/2 hour unpacking and re-shoeing job, we were again off toward Bucks Lakes. We finally arrived at a perfect campsite above the lake with pasture enough for all.

We quickly turned all the horses loose except Shab who was picketed on a fifty-foot rope. We set up camp and prepared the fire to ready the barbecue for the New York steaks. However, Cord and Chuck decided between the two of them to disappear until the next afternoon. Always secretive, they would not reveal their whereabouts.

The following morning we were greeted by a crisp, cool dawn as we prepared our fishing gear to catch our breakfast. By the time we hiked to the lake, a light breeze began to pick up. We climbed the massive rocks on the east shore to get a good vantage point. Neither Ron nor I had any luck with salmon eggs, night crawlers, or red worms. The breeze was getting to be too much to fight, although the air temperature was warming up.

That afternoon we took a short ride up Bucks Meadow Canyon looking for water to fill our canteens. This was such a dry year it was really difficult to find good water to drink. We finally found a good spot to get our water but it still had to be purified. This was where those shifty brothers turned up. They just walked out of the woods as if they had been on a stroll in their backyard.

Our evening campfire and cook fire were not easy to start as there was very little dead wood to be found. After a good workout locating fuel, we soon had a fire going and our pot of boiling water for the lobster was on. The raspberry cobbler for dessert was just perfect.

The following morning we packed up after another uneventful attempt at fishing. All of our red worms had died, but we still had over 20 night-crawlers left. We set out for Emigrant Lake about 11AM and arrived at the summit overlooking the lake about noon. The view was beyond description. The lake was encased in granite with the sun glistening off the water and rock alike. We made our way down the narrow rocky trail to the east end of the lake where we found abundant pasture for the horses and plenty of campsites to choose from.

We found a perfect camp with a tremendous view. The only problem was the wind. This was no longer a breeze, but a wind and at 9500' that was a cold wind. After dark, the wind subsided until a just few hours after sunrise. We decided to postpone the fishing until morning. At first light, Ron woke us all up to go fishing.

There was no wind, and we were hoping that it would stay that way. Well, it stayed calm until 9:30, but we were still unable to get even a little bite. Well, we would try later. We decided to hike or rock climb the small mountain of boulders rising up from behind our camp. The first part was easy, although I had to stop repeatedly. There was just too little oxygen at that elevation. We finally came to a point where we had to climb the sheer face of the rock. None of us felt foolhardy enough to try that. We then returned to camp to relax before dinner, although I really was expecting Chuck to try it.

Dinner was kept light just to be different. Steak sandwiches and French fries would be our fast food. We decided to do a day trip from this base camp tomorrow. We wanted to fish Emigrant Meadow Lake and do some sight seeing.

We rose at sunrise to a beautiful morning. It had been cold that night as we had ice on top of our water. We ate a leisurely breakfast before we set out on the day's adventure. We headed up the trail fork that went to Mosquito Pass. The trees soon gave way to a windswept plain littered with massive boulders. The view down toward Kennedy Meadows and Sonora Pass was magnificent. The geology changes dramatically north of this point.

We descended from this lofty perch and headed to a trail junction at Lunch Meadow where we stopped for lunch. After lunch, we turned north toward Brown Bear Pass. This was a climb of 1000' and at 10,000' the horses took it slowly. The trail was treacherous as it had been littered with rock and scree from many rock slides. At one point we had to climb off of our horses and pick our way through the rubble. Cord managed to lead us through this trail that was nearly impossible with the mountain of loose rock rising straight up on our left side and the sheer drop-off of several hundred feet to our right. The trail wound up this mountainside to the pass, on what appeared to be an old road or wagon tread that was about six feet wide at best.

At the top, we were rewarded with a spectacular view of Emigrant Meadow and its associated lake, which was so far down in size because of the dry year it could have been called a pond. Cord was nowhere in sight. There were boulders with loose rock just waiting for us on the descent to the basin. Most of the time we could not see more than a hundred feet in front of us on the trail.

It happened very suddenly. I was struggling in the rear with my saddle horse and my pack horse, when we began to hear rock falling. My horses began dancing and I heard shouts from the others struggling with their steeds. We then heard many shots in rapid fire coming from somewhere. Within minutes, everything had returned to normal. I was struck by several large rocks with one of them injuring my right leg. The Wood brothers pack horse, Joe, had broken a leg and had to be put down. This was bad, but not as bad as what was to come. We packed up all we could on my pack horse and distributed the rest among the remaining horses.

We continued morosely down the trail saying nothing to no one. Chuck rounded a sharp bend a large boulder when he began shouting. I could make out "Cord" and thought that he had been injured in the same rock slide. He hadn't. It was far worse. He had been mauled by a very large black bear protecting her cubs. Cord had lost a lot of blood and was in a lot of pain. He had managed to kill the she-bear with five rounds from his .44

magnum. How many hit her, we never found out. Cord was bandaged up and placed on a litter.

The trail back to camp was relatively easy considering all that had happened. We headed down the trail past Middle Emigrant Lake and followed the north fork of Cherry Creek to Blackbird Lake and then back down to Emigrant Lake. As we were crossing the meadow toward camp, we passed a pack outfit of about twenty horses. The last horse in their string was dragging a long lead rope. It was my horse Whiskey! He had untied himself and was going home with them. Fortunately, he recognized us and so he was easy to catch. We explained our situation to the leader of the pack outfit and he agreed to take Cord and Chuck back out to medical help. We found out later that it took them a whole day to reach help at Kennedy Meadows. Cord was taken out to a hospital in Reno by helicopter. After several months of recovering, he is now as bizarre as ever. But now, back to our story in the wilderness.

All the campsites at this end of the lake were now taken. Our retreat had grown infested with people. Crevices in rocks were found to contain various bits of trash from propane gas cylinders to empty gallon jugs of Gallo wine to a tennis shoe. We packed up what we could carry, but a lot had to be left behind.

The following morning, we packed up and left right after breakfast. We stopped at the lake on the way out to try our luck at fishing again, but we were unsuccessful. We continued on down the trail back to Buck's Lake to cross it at its isthmus and head down to Wood Lake. At the isthmus between upper and lower Buck Lakes, we encountered a group of about 40 college students on a wilderness adventure of their own. Within a half hour, we reached what we thought was Wood Lake. After carefully surveying the area, we concluded that it was Wood Lake, but due to the drought, it was much smaller than normal. Shab was left picketed while the others grazed on the grass bordering the lake.

We set up camp in a large, well-used packer's camp. We tried fishing, but even our night-crawlers were dead. Pat found a large grub which he put on a hook and tossed out. Still, nothing wanted it. We quit fishing and we left the lines in the water and went back to camp for dinner.

We used the last of the hamburger to make Sloppy Joes. They were delicious on the remains of our loaves of sourdough bread. The horses had wandered to the far side of the little lake by this time. Ron was getting edgy and I was no longer so sure of the wisdom of letting the horses graze freely. I slowly got up and went to bring them back.

As soon as I got back, I heard Ron yelling and ran up to see what all the commotion was about. Ron had found a good sized trout on the end of his line. It had gone for a portion of the grub. There really were fish in here! We all got excited and tried fishing again with no more luck. We decided to leave our lines in the water with a piece of grub on the hooks overnight.

The following morning we rose quickly to turn the horses loose and to check out our lines. We found two more pan-sized trout for our breakfast. We soon had hash-brown potatoes and the fish cooking. Ron then noticed our horses crossing the creek on the far side of the lake. I again walked after them. This time rather than stopping they continued back along down the trail to our last camp. I was in a slow run by this time. I cut across a dry pond bed and then cross-country to head them off. I came out at a point about 3 feet above the trail. I had cut them off. The horses were coming toward me as I jumped down to the trail. I slipped and fell hitting my head against a tree or a soft rock. The next thing I knew, there was Chickadee looking down at me asking if I was OK. Caught her! I love it when a plan comes together. I rode Hassani and led Chickadee with Whiskey following. As I neared camp, Pat rode up on Shab to see what had become of me. I then began sneezing and sneezing and sneezing. This didn't stop for three days.

We finished breakfast and packed up. Just as we were leaving, another party of six on foot moved in. We said hello and exchanged pleasantries with them, then we headed for an all day ride down Buck Meadow Creek to Groundhog Meadow passing through Louse Canyon. At the meadow, we had come full circle for this trip.

We had only several miles to go before we reached Grouse Lake. We wanted to find our old campsite, but we couldn't find it. The campground was full to overflowing with people either camping, visiting, or passing through. We set up camp in an out of the way spot.

This spot began to look familiar to each of us more and more. We finally came to the dumbfounded realization that this was the campsite we had been looking for all along. After this revelation, I lay back and took a short nap until dinner time, while Ron and Pat went swimming in the lake.

While Pat was beginning dinner and campfire, I went exploring the realm beyond our camp. About ten minutes after I had left, I heard the sound of gunfire. I hurried back in the direction of camp. As I approached camp, I heard Ron laughing with Pat yelling something indecipherable. Then I heard

"YOU did it!"

"What?"

"Where were you?" queried Ron.

Apparently, someone or something had put live ammunition in our campfire ring. Practical joke? Is the wilderness now so close to "civilization" that these jokers can destroy our wilderness heritage? Dinner was eaten in silence, except for my sneezing and Pat's yelling at me to stop.

We packed up and left early, anxious to be out on the trail and away from the crowd. We soon encountered hikers and equestrians too numerous to remember. The ride out of Grouse Lake to Crabtree Camp seemed much longer than the ride in. We rode in to the trailhead about noon. I found a dollar bill stuck in my vent window with no note. Everything was locked up and nothing was found missing. It's a strange world we live in.

For next year's trip we will be in Yosemite National Park below Yosemite Valley. We hope to avoid the crowds and enjoy, once again, the peace and solitude of a Wilderness Adventure.

Chapter 4

This year we were going to traverse a course through magnificent southern Yosemite National Park. We were well prepared this year. We got together a day early to shop, pack, and prepare ourselves for this Wilderness Adventure. Even with all the extra time to prepare, we still did not reach the trailhead at Mono Meadows until a little after eight PM. By nine we were all saddled up and ready to hit the trail. The sun was down and it was getting dark.

After several false starts (we kept forgetting small things), we on our way. We had a minimum of three miles to get away from the trailhead to comply with park regulations. The trail cut across a mountainside studded with gigantic trees. We could barely make out the shape of the trees through the deepening darkness of night. All of a sudden I heard Pat cry out. After the cussing had died down, we found out that he had run into a tree and was dehorsed down the mountainside. It was too dark to see any of the action. We paused again while we dug out the flashlights. Even with the little light we could barely make out anything off the trail much less find a campsite. After being on the trail for 30-40 minutes we began in earnest to find a place to camp. This was not going to be easy. We couldn't see a thing, but soon we had stopped and unpacked and began setting up camp. We didn't know how far we had come, but it was definitely not three miles. We would get up really early and head out before a ranger could find us.

The next morning it took only a few minutes to gather the horses. We were saddled up and ready to hit the trail within forty five minutes. After thirty five minutes on the trail, we lost it. We thought we were on it until it petered out along the river. This was Champ's first year at packing. So far he had been doing well. The packs were weighed in at close to 300 pounds. He was learning very quickly to negotiate the tight quarters as we edged up the river. Finally it became apparent that even we couldn't proceed any farther. We retraced our steps to where we first encountered the river. Now it looked like this was a ford. The river was about 150 feet wide so there wasn't any concern regarding the current. The bank was fairly steep, climbing about 100 feet up out of the river. We hit that and began to run up to the top.

This was when I noticed that the packs were not quite even on Champ. We stopped here and redid the packs and checked the map. We were still at 6800 foot elevation. The big climb would come later in the week as we planned to scale Fernandez and Red Rock Pass at better than 11,000 feet. We finished up our snacks and set out again. The packs were still not quite right, but they were close enough for now.

The trail gently rose along a sloping canyon wall with Illilouette Creek down below us on our right. We crossed several creeklets and one ten foot wide boggy area. My horse, Whiskey, crossed with no trouble, but Champ balked and nearly pulled me out of the saddle. I finally dropped the rope and turned Whiskey around. There was Champ staring at that small pool of mud. Whiskey then refused to cross it again until I convinced him that it would be a lot easier on him if he would do what I wanted. We crossed the bog and picked up the rope and proceeded once again to cross. Again Champ refused. Whiskey and I were about to cross back, when for no reason, Whiskey leaped high and wide across the mud hole right into a large pine tree.

Just before we hit it he changed directions leaving me glued to the tree. Champ took off down the trail away from us.

I caught up to him in no time and soon had him up to the bog. After a little coaxing he jumped it. I had to walk through the mess. I caught Whiskey and again we were off. I was tired at this point and it was only a little after noon. We pushed on for another hour and a half until we came to a nice stream flowing rapidly down to the Illilouette below. It was in the mid-eighties and a hazy, but cloudless, day. This was not only a perfect site for lunch, but would also serve as camp for tonight as Pat was again feeling a little altitude sickness at 7000 feet.

We began preparing lunch and camp simultaneously. Soon the smell of barbecued ribs permeated the air. We sat drinking our ice-cold Cokes just enjoying the beautiful day. I decided to take a nap. I woke up about five. Groggily I looked around and I couldn't find anyone. I could see the horses grazing peacefully up the hillside from me. My two horses were loose while the other two were on thirty-foot ropes.

Pat and Ron had gone exploring, but soon returned. They told me about the terrific view up the mountain we were camped on. I followed them up the slope for the next thirty minutes. The view from this rock capped mountain was every much as beautiful as they had described it to me.

We hiked back to camp to prepare our gourmet feast. Tonight we would dine on tacos and enchiladas. We had plenty of Coke to go along with our meal. As soon as it got dark I went to bed.

We were up early again, but didn't pack up and leave until ten. After several hours of climbing, we reached Merced Pass.

Champ's packs were slipping again. We needed a break and had to readjust the packs. Besides, we all needed a Coke.

We had just begun loosening the cinches on the pack, when four backpackers snuck up behind us and spooked all of us. We exchanged pleasantries, then they left. We re-seated the pack saddle. We were joking about following those women back-down the hill. I didn't think that was a good idea as they were probably better fit than we were. We decided to drink our Coke.

Out of nowhere appeared eight more backpackers. Did they hear us? Were they going to kill us for our comments or our Cokes? They said "Hello" and one of them commented that she would bet that we had cold cokes inside. We laughed nervously. We played the ritual out and the savages left us. What an ordeal. Two of them looked like the Hulk. We split a can and quickly saddled up to escape. Just as we were leaving we came across another small pack of these women backpackers. They stayed clear of us as we warily rode past.

We had only a few miles to go before we reached Moraine Meadows. It was a gradual, leisurely descent from the pass. The forests and views were beautiful, but hazy. Everything appeared so dry. This was going to be a short ride today of only six miles. Champ had been lagging behind and the packs just kept slipping off to the side. I was sure that his back was getting sore. We reached Moraine Meadows only to find no water. There was plenty of grass and several good campsites, but no water.

We stopped for a lunch break and reset the pack on Champ. This was getting old and I was getting frustrated. Ron and Pat had about had it with me and my horse. We continued on toward Chain Lakes. We began climbing again. After another few hours we had reached lower Chain Lake at 9500 feet. It was a beautiful lake perched at the edge of a sharp drop. There was a large meadow at the inlet to the lake.

We rode into a perfect campsite and unpacked the horses. Camp was quickly established. The view from the kitchen was magnificent, looking out over the crystal clear lake to the majestic mountains in the distance shrouded in wisps of fiery clouds. Our tents were set up off of the granite kitchen, about 75 feet away. The horses were grazing peacefully in the waning light. My two were again left loose, but tonight they would use the cowbell. The cowbell has such an annoying clang, but it lets you easily find your horses; That is, if they are moving.

We quickly prepared our dinner while we set up the gas lantern. This day had sure gone fast. We covered four extra miles, but it seemed to be at a snails pace. I was worried about Champ's back. It was tender to the touch, but not bad. Give him a day or two and he would be back to normal. The other horses were in fine shape. The food was excellent. It was too bad we didn't have maid service. We were too tired after the long day and the large portion of steak and potatoes we just consumed to do anything else.

We were up bright and early. It was a cold morning. There was ice on everything, including my sleeping bag. I put my horses on the ropes and freed the others. When I got back, Pat had a fire going. Breakfast was served in no time. We discussed the condition of the pack horse and decided to ride the Red Rock Pass - Fernandez Pass loop tomorrow and keep Champ tethered in the pasture of plenty. Today we would hang out around the Chain Lakes area.

I set out climbing the rocks behind our campsite. I became winded quickly. I rested a lot. Before I realized it, I was looking down at the lake below and behind me, barely visible, was the glimmer of Middle Chain Lakes. It was an awe inspiring sight. I could picture where Upper Chain Lakes would be in the huge glaciated basin ahead and above me. I sunbathed for a while enjoying the peace and quiet. I then hiked over to the trail and almost fell into someone's camp. I snuck away and went back to camp along the trail.

Later that afternoon we rode up to Upper Chain Lake and found its small sloped campsite occupied by six people. It was only a five mile ride in from their trailhead at Chiquito Pass. We filled our canteens from the lake as this was the purest water we had seen on this trip. We rode back to camp to prepare our feast.

While unpacking I found that we didn't have the steaks we bought. We also didn't have any hamburger. What else could we have forgotten? Tempers were wearing thin. Oh No! We also forgot to pack my special precooked elk stew. No wonder we had room for thirty-six cans of Coke. We were missing most of our food. What were we to do. We started by blaming each other. It was a riot now that we look back upon it. Even then it took us several hours to realize that it was everyone's fault. Our teamwork in preparing and packing for this trip was sadly lacking.

In planning this route I had swung us near an exit to Wawona which could resupply us with Coca Cola. This was a 3000 foot drop, so it was only intended as an emergency. Also it would be very, very expensive. I had no idea that we would need to resupply our ice chest with food.

Our evening meal of noodles, ketchup, and some kind of freeze dried food was all we had that night. While eating in silence, we began to hear a high pitched keening coming from across the miniature lake. It didn't sound like any animal that we had ever heard before. I got up to check on the horses who were picketed on thirty foot ropes in the middle of the lush meadow.

By the time I reached them the wailing had stopped, but I couldn't find Pat's horse Shab. It was getting dark and he is a dark bay. I shouted to the others, but I was too far from camp for them to hear me. I quickly started back to camp, but at 9500 feet I just as quickly slowed down to catch my breath. When I got to camp there was no one there. Where had they gone???

The wailing started up again and now I could hear a horse or horses whinnying for all they were worth. The horse sounds were coming from where I just left the horses. I walked back to the horses, but now Champ was missing. His picket and rope was all that was left. It was then that I heard a lot of shouting from up the trail.

At this point I was afraid to leave the horses, so I gathered the two remaining horses and headed back to camp. As I approached camp I could see a large, dark object in the middle of camp. I stopped dead in my tracks, peering intensely at whatever it was. The horses weren't excited, so I finally decided that it wasn't a bear. I moved closer. It was rummaging through our packs. What was that thing? All at once it dawned on me. It was Champ helping himself to what was left of our meager rations. I caught him and proceeded to tie them all up to the picket line strung between two trees.

Just as I sat down in camp I heard the brush rustling behind me. It was Ron and Pat returning to camp after looking for the source of the wailing. They wanted to know where I went, so I quickly told them about Shab. Pat began to laugh and said he moved Shab earlier to the other side of camp. I wasted a good worry. I then hit the sack and was soon asleep.

We were up early as we had to make about twelve miles that day. We had a small breakfast and were on the trail by nine AM. The ride was beautiful and uneventful. We passed the ranger station about noon and found a lone backpacker waiting for the ranger. We pushed on through steaming jungle.

We soon came to little Johnson Lake. It was much smaller than usual because of the drought conditions. We stopped to reset the pack on Champs back. It kept slipping to the left, leaving Champ with a tender area on his back. The packs had been carefully weighed to within several pounds of each other. I knew that if we didn't correct the problem we were going to be without a pack horse very soon. We repacked and headed off to Crescent Lake a mere one and a half miles away.

Soon the packs had slipped again, but we pushed on. Only a little longer. Champ was lagging farther and farther behind. It seemed to take forever to reach the lake. We set up camp, then proceeded to take a hike around this nearly dry lake. It was situated on the edge of the high country overlooking the south fork of the Merced River 4000 feet below. What a view of this canyon and the majestic peaks beyond. We sat in silence on this precipitous point. There wasn't a cloud in the sky. Soon, beyond one of the tallest peaks across from us a cloud began billowing up. It very quickly became an enormous mushroom-shaped cloud towering above that stately peak. Still there were no clouds anywhere except that one. Was it a nuclear blast from a test site in Nevada? As it reached a certain altitude the wind tore off the top of the mushroom, but the cloud kept rising to meet the wind. Maybe it was a magic mushroom cloud.

After an hour of this we hiked back on the boggy, shaded side of the lake. The mosquitoes were horrendous. In the 45 minutes it took to get back to camp, I had been bitten at least a dozen times, perhaps more. We had a frugal dinner and went to sleep.

We rose early and prepared our scant breakfast. We were extra careful to weigh the packs and ensure that they were placed on Champ's back properly. We were off. Within thirty minutes we had to stop and reset the packs. This was getting old, and both Pat and Ron were getting more and more impatient. This pattern continued for the next six miles.

We finally came to an old leveled building site with only the concrete foundation remaining. There was another horse group there so we continued down the trail. Champ was slowing down as his back got sorer. We stopped and looked at the map, and it looked like the camp back up the trail was the best spot to stop. We turned back and arrived at the camp.

The other people were packing up and getting ready to leave. Ron wanted to continue on to Wawona, but I explained to him that the five to six miles would be too much for the pack horse. Tempers were wearing thin. Ron wanted to go ahead without me or the pack horse, but we finally resolved our differences and set up camp.

Across the trail through the trees was a long meadow of wildflowers and grass. Hassani and Shab were picketed, with Whiskey and Champ turned loose with a cow bell attached to one of them. The bell didn't last long over the protests of noise pollution. The horses didn't care. They were in heaven.

Our camp was several hundred feet above the river below, so we had to hike down the rocks or walk down the trail for a hundred yards to get water. We spent the rest of the afternoon hiking up this boulder strewn river. It was fun and relaxing, but we didn't find any artifacts or gold nuggets.

We ate the last of our freeze dried food. We still had Cokes left and we enjoyed them. After dinner we went to check on the horses. At the southern end of the meadow, hidden in the trees, we found the old building that had once sat on the building site we were camped on. We suspected that it once belonged to a sheepherder around the turn of the century.

Just as we reached camp, a pack string of about twenty horses went by on the way to Wawona. This was about eight thirty and it was beginning to get dark. The gal leading the train said it was about a two to three hour ride to Wawona. Well, that is not a long ride but to negotiate a 4000 foot drop in the dark..... Need I say more?

Just about sunrise I heard another pack string going down the trail. I stayed in my sleeping bag for another hour or so. I kept thinking about Champ and Whiskey who were still loose. I was hoping they wouldn't follow the pack string. I finally got up to check on them. It took fifteen minute to reach Shab and Hassani who were at the far end of the meadow. There was no sign of my horses. I headed back to camp with Shab and Hassani.

I began saddling Hassani as Pat and Ron got up and began heating water for breakfast. I told them my horses were gone and that I was going out to look for them. Hassani kept dancing and trying to look over his back toward the canyon wall across the river opposite our camp. What was he looking at? We started off down the trail. Something was definitely bothering him. I finally saw it. About three hundred yards up the sheer rock wall of the facing canyon were my horses. What were they doing up there? How did they get there? Did the think they were mountain goats? It was all rock. There was no grass. I had to dismount and hike toward them. Fortunately they met me halfway. Ron and Pat had another good laugh.

We were all anxious to get to Wawona, so we left camp about eight. We had decided to find a spot off the trail to unload all our gear so Champ would only have to carry a load on the way back. We began searching at the trail junction. One trail went down to Wawona while the other went on to Turner Meadows.

Pat lead the way. We rode around brush, trees, boulders, and through old campsites. After ten minutes or more he finally found a remote, secure site to leave our things. It didn't take long to unload, but it took longer to find our way out of the well-hidden spot. When we reached the trail, I took the lead.

We had ridden no more than two minutes when I spotted some backpacker's camp right alongside the trail. What idiot would camp right on the trail? It took all of us several minute to realize that this was no backpacker's camp, but our own hidden cache. Terrific! We kept riding and left everything where it was.

We began the descent to Wawona. It was a spectacular, easy trail. We reached the bottom in a little over an hour and found the store twenty minutes later. After we bought all that we could afford (they wouldn't take Ron's body), we left with several steaks, Coke, and junk food. Ron said he quit drinking on this trip, so he had a root beer. Pat had several beers and I had ice-cold Coke. We had purchased submarine sandwiches as well and proceeded to scarf them down in the shade of the Sequoias outside the store.

The trip back up the mountain only took a little over an hour and the ride was uneventful. We reached our temporary camp and loaded everything up. We then headed out to Turner Meadows about four miles away. We reached the upper end of the meadows within an hour.

It seemed to be miles long and about 300 yards wide. It took us another hour to find a suitable campsite, but it was great. We set up camp and then I turned the horses loose to graze to their hearts' content.

We found a narrow, deep creek running though the meadow. The creek was at most two feet wide and about three feet deep. That got Ron very excited. FISH! Sure enough, he caught several good-sized trout. We put off eating the steaks until the next night. The fish were terrific. What an enjoyable evening! It had taken us this long to get used to each other again. Things were looking good.

We ate half of our sausage and eggs for breakfast. We had a six mile ride to Lost Bear Meadow, where we would spend our last night and feast on our steaks. We reached the far side of the meadow in about two hours. This side was marshy and tree studded. The trail went completely around the meadow, so we took the right fork hoping to find a site.

Soon our trail turned into an obvious snowmobile trail complete with metal markers up the trees. We later found out that there used to be a ski lodge back up the trail at Ostrander Lake. At this point we entered "The Burn." A recent fire had ravaged both sides of the trail, including the meadow we planned to camp in. We studied the map again and decided that because it was noon we would stop at the trail junction ahead and have lunch.

At the junction we again looked at the map and realized that we were only three miles away from our trailhead. After debating the situation, we all decided to eat our steaks here and head back to the truck. Pat started a small fire and soon we had our steaks cooking away. While they were cooking, several hikers went by and commented on our meal. Some were astonished that we would be cooking fresh meat in the wilderness. We couldn't understand their amazement. What was so amazing about three dirty, ragged horsemen eating a dead cow in the wilderness? Didn't our forefathers do it this way? If they could, so could we.

After thoroughly snuffing our fire, we packed up and were off. The burn became much worse. Soon we reached the highway. Now we had a problem. We had to stay on the trail, but there was no trail back to our trailhead. All we had was the Glacier Point highway for a mile, and we weren't allowed to have the horses on the road. We did the best we could. Why couldn't the Park Service add a simple trail following the highway? That should take less thought and money than to construct a separate horse and dog trail at Castle Crags State Park. They have plenty of rangers to check you for your permit.

This year we had not only the wilderness and park regulations to contend with, but also our forgetfulness and our personalities to overcome. Next year will be Pat's turn to plan a trip. It will be much better. We all hope that the drought will be over.

Chapter 5

I had just recently moved to northeastern California when I met Jan Creighton. She had asked me to assist her in putting up flags for an endurance ride she was sponsoring. Mary Wortman was also in this group and the three of us began talking about riding the entire length of the (P)acific (C)rest (T)rail in segments each year. We began riding short stretches of that trail near the Fall River Valley and became increasingly excited about such an adventure. We decided to ride first in September the segment of trail from Castle Crags State Park on I-5 to Red Mountain where we would leave the trail and ride fourteen miles to Jan's ranch in Dana. The ride was to be 75 miles total, so we allocated three days for the trip.

We were on the trail by eight AM at an elevation of 2100'. The morning was warm and it quickly got hotter as the day wore on. We spent a good deal of the day climbing Girard Ridge on its south facing slopes with swarms of flies all around us. The heat was almost unbearable. There was very little grass along the trail and only a few creeks, but there was plenty of water for the horses. The trail was in excellent condition and we made good time. We were planning on camping at the Ah-Di-Na campground (site of Hearst's hunting lodge) along the McCloud River. We had a long 28 miles that first day before making camp.

We arrived at the campground after a grueling ten hours in the saddle. The campground was surrounded by an apple orchard and the creek was infested with blackberries. There was more than enough fruit for man and beast alike. We even had toilets nearby. What a life! However, there was a large sign posted in the outhouse:

WARNING!

BEARS

Now that sounded ominous. Why the outhouse? The sign also advised to lock all food in your vehicle which was not an easy task with horses. There were also heavy garbage cans with bear-proof lids. We retired at dark as we were in for another long day tomorrow. Just then, Mary's horse began to colic.

After walking her mare for twenty minutes, the symptoms subsided and we again tried to fall asleep. I was rudely awakened by shouts just as I had drifted off to sleep.

BEARS!!

I sat up reaching for my flashlight. All the flashlight could do for us was to show us that the bear was as big as the picnic table he was standing next to. He was content eating something and at the moment it was not us. Mary had tied a short leash on her dog, Ben, which was tied securely to the end of her sleeping bag. Ben was going crazy. He wanted to kill that bear and kept struggling against the weight of Mary's sleeping bag. If Ben had been any larger, he would have dragged Mary with him after the bear. There was also another bear out of my flashlight's tiny beam of light. All we could see of it were the two burning embers that were his eyes. Jan and Mary's horses were having an attack of happy feet, while my horse, Pete, just continued eating away. The bears didn't seem to bother him at all. Since Jan and Mary were awake and watching the bears watch us, I decided to go back to sleep.

Morning came far too soon for all of us. The bears had left, but I found the item that had interested them so much during the night. It was my leather banana bag that had held my apple-newton bars and coconut oil suntan lotion. They had ripped it to shreds. I had to figure out a way to repack my gear, which was not an easy task. Fortunately, that was the worst that happened to us. We let the horses eat for a few hour, then we were off on the next leg of our journey.

The trail started off in good repair, but we soon came to a 15 mile stretch that had a lot of deadfall across the trail. We were also climbing from Ah-Di-Na's 2200' to Grizzly Peak at 6300'. We kept switch-backing in and out of gullies that generally had a little water in them. The scenery was beautiful, although it was not very spectacular. By afternoon our forest cover had shrunk in size and silver -tipped firs began making their appearance. We knew that we were getting close to the top. However, we still had a long way to go. The deadfall was a real challenge as the slopes we were traversing were steep. The twenty miles we were to cover that day felt more like fifty after fighting with all the deadfall. We finally reached the top and encountered a trail maintenance crew who were in the process of clearing the trail ahead of us around Grizzly Peak. They opened their ice chest and offered each of us an ice-cold Coke. I had been dreaming of one since we left yesterday morning. That was great and the views from this saddle were tremendous.

After we finished our Cokes, we continued along the freshly cleared trail. Soon we were on the south slope of the mountain. The trail had been blasted out of rock. There was a

3000' drop to Devil's Canyon below us and nothing but rock above us. Jan was watching the trail closely because of the large bear tracks we had spotted. If we came across a bear, there was no place to go. The same was true of a backpacker. The trail was a mere 36 inches wide. We just hoped that neither animal would appear. Our luck held out and we finally made it to the Grizzly Peak fire road which we descended to Stout's Meadow a short half mile away.

Stout's Meadow was a large beautiful meadow with plenty of water. There were several snow survey buildings on the meadow's edge. We established camp near one of the buildings next to a small creek. It was an ideal campsite. The only level spots were in the vast meadow, so we laid our sleeping bags and ground cloths out at the edge of the meadow. By morning we were all thoroughly soaked from the moisture. We learned from that experience never to sleep in an open meadow.

After we dried out and got warmed up, we packed up and hit the trail. We still had about 33 miles to go before we would reach our evening's destination. The first 19 miles went quickly and we stopped for lunch just before we were to exit the PCT near Kemp Flat before Red Mountain. Our food supply was running low, so we shared our remaining food.

The next fourteen miles tested our endurance. We had all ridden this same stretch many times before, so there was no new scenery to divert our attention. At one point, where we had stopped for a break, I was climbing back into the saddle and then, because of a lack of strength, I fell off the other side and landed on my head. I was really getting tired! We finally reached Jan's ranch in Dana about dusk. That last fourteen miles was the longest fourteen miles I had ever ridden.

Next year we planned to ride a part of the PCT from Castle Crags State Park north to Scott Mountain Summit. We knew now how to pack more gear and how far we could travel on a good trail such as the PCT. This had been a great experience for the three of us and we were really looking forward to next years adventure.

Chapter 6

    This year Jan, Mary, and I had decided to continue our PCT trek from Castle Crags State Park located on I-5 north of Redding. This year, however, we were going to ride the trail north instead of south as we had last year. It was early in September and the day was already warm as we saddled up. Our starting point was at 2300' and we had a climb of 4500' ahead of us before we would drop into Seven Lakes Basin for camp that evening. As the day wore on the temperature would climb into the 100's, and the flies would swarm mercilessly around our heads.

    We had contacted the park rangers and they had left the locked gate open for us at the beginning of the trail. We rode under the cover of incense cedars and big-leaf maple trees during much of the morning as we went in and out of dry gullies. There was no grass to speak of, although there was quite a profusion of poison oak. We soon came to the Dog Trail where we were supposed to send our dogs, but we couldn't take our horses on that trail. We had to stay on the horse trail with the horses but the dogs weren't allowed on that trail. We wondered what idiot thought this rule up. We decided that the dogs really were small horses, so they followed us up the horse trail.

    Shortly after we had resolved this dilemma, we began climbing. We began a series of numerous switch-backs in and out of gullies with dry freshets. We finally came to a refreshing creek near the trail which still had adequate water for all of us. This was the last water we would find until we left the PCT for Seven Lakes Basin about twelve miles ahead. The views of the crags were tremendous and forever changing. Right after we refreshed ourselves in the freshet, we began our most strenuous climb, about 500' in less than one mile. When we reached the crest we left the live oaks below us as well as those annoying flies.

We continued our climb in the partial shade of Douglas firs and sugar pines, again weaving in and out of dry gullies. Some of the gullies had damp ground in spots and that was where we first noticed the pitcher plants. These cobra-shaped plants derive part of their nutritional requirements by devouring flies and other small insects. It was too bad there weren't a lot more of them back down the trail to feast on the horde of flies. This interesting plant is found primarily in the Klamath Mountains, though it is sometimes found in a few choice places elsewhere. They apparently thrive in boggy, serpentine soils which is found in abundance in these mountains.

At one point, we could have descended northwest cross-country to Scott Camp Creek to nearly level terrain and set up our camp, but it appeared much too steep for our horses, so we rode on. This stretch of trail gave us magnificent views both north and south as we straddled the mountain's crest. Soon we could see Echo Lake below us to the south at the base of Boulder Peak. We continued riding for another hour before the trail veered southwest and Upper Seven Lake grabbed our attention below us in a large glaciated basin. We had to continue riding to the Trinity Divide at 6800' before we came to an old jeep trail that descended nearly 1400' to the lake below. To say that this road was steep would be a gross understatement. We had ridden a total of thirty miles today. We were tired and so were the horses.

Camp was set up in a matter of minutes. I had brought my folding backpacker's fishing rod and reel and I was ready to try my luck at fishing. Due to all the bouncing around in the pack, the line on the reel had become severely tangled. It took me the rest of the evening to untangle it, so I was unable to fish that night. That night we dined on freeze-dried enchiladas and apple d'light.

Morning came far too early for me, but I got up quickly to untie Cedar, my 20-year-old Quarter Horse gelding, and start fishing. This time I was able to get my line into the water, but couldn't get it back out. It snagged on some creature lurking in the depths. I went back to camp and ate freeze-dried Western Omelet and drank my chocolate milk. These freeze-dried foods were a lot better tasting than the ones I was used to in the sixties.

After breakfast, we saddled up and started out for another long day in the saddle. I climbed on Cedar and I could tell right off that something was wrong. He didn't want to move. He was tired. That long ride yesterday had taken a lot out of him. I had to walk him up that steep jeep road to the trail. That climb up was something else. I was thoroughly exhausted long before we reached the top. Once on top, I climbed back on Cedar and we were off. The views on this crest were fantastic. We had views of the Trinity River drainage below us to the southwest and the Sacramento River drainage below us to the northeast. The trail was in perfect shape as it continued straddling the crest.

We were all feeling the effects of yesterday's ride. By lunch time we had decided that we would camp at Toad Lake for the night, even though it would mean that we had only ridden six miles for the day. We continued on after lunch, enjoying the beautiful scenery, knowing that we only had a few miles left ahead. Soon we came to a spur trail that went to Porcupine Lake, which was only a third of a mile away. We decided to visit this lake and see if it had a camp for us. The beauty of this lake was indescribable. There was a small camp, but there was no grass in this glaciated basin that the lake was nestled in. Porcupine Lake was well worth the visit.

Toad Lake was only a half mile away off the PCT on an old trail, 6W06, that was not in the best of condition, but still very easy to follow to Toad Lake below. This was a much bigger lake than Porcupine or Upper Seven Lakes. There was plenty of grass and numerous places to camp. We found a nice campsite with a picnic table and set up camp. Although the PCT avoided the meadows and lakes, the old trails didn't. We could understand the Forest Service wanting to preserve these fragile areas, but who are they preserving them for?? Since the PCT was to be designed for equestrians, why did they avoid all the lakes and meadows?

After camp I went down to the water's edge and once again spent an hour untangling my line from the reel. I cast the line out and within a minute I had a fish. I tried to reel it in, but the line had become tangled once again. I spent twenty minutes fixing it and then reeled in my fish. I spent the next two hours losing all my weights and hooks to snags without catching any more fish. The rest of the day I spent relaxing. After dinner, we hiked around the lake enjoying the serenity of the beautiful evening.

By morning we were all feeling rested, including Cedar. He was ready to get moving and see new sights. As we left the lake, we took trail 6W06 out of the Toad Lake basin the opposite way we had come in and rejoined the PCT a little further down the trail from where we had left it yesterday. The old trail was almost like a deer trail climbing out of that basin. A few miles farther down the trail, we came to a trail junction with the Sisson-Callahan trail that came up from Lake Siskiyou near Mt. Shasta City. The views from this trail junction were fantastic. We were on top of the world at 8000'. The Sisson-Callahan trail descended off either side of this windy saddle to excellent places to camp with unlimited meadows for the horses. We continued on the PCT toward Deadfall Lakes.

We first came upon disappointing Lower Deadfall Lake just as we exited the cover of a red fir forest that we had been riding through for the last mile or so. This small, shallow lake was about a few hundred yards below the trail surrounded by pieces of crumbled granite so large that it was impassable to our horses. Upper Deadfall Lake was a lot better and only a few hundred yards ahead. It was large and deep and was off on a short spur trail about fifty yards away. We stopped here for a short break and to admire the beautiful lake and the reflection of Mt. Eddy which towered above. There was grass and several perfect places to camp, but we were not ready to stop so soon. We were planning on making it to Bull Lake, which was about twelve more miles away, before we made camp.

After leaving Deadfall Lakes, we crossed another old trail that went back over Mt. Eddy and then down to that old desperado trail, the Sisson-Callahan Trail. We continued on, passing two confusing junctions of the trail where there was faint tread going off with old PCT signs on the trees. We guessed that the temporary PCT had once taken a different route than the new permanent freeway-like trail and someone had neglected to remove the old signs. We soon crossed well-traveled Parks Creek Road which descended fourteen miles northeast to I-5, about three miles west of Weed. We passed many ephemeral creeklets and came to a small meadow where we stopped to have lunch. The springs that fed this meadow form the headwaters of the Trinity River. The weather had been warm and dry, so at this elevation of 7000' it was perfect.

After lunch we passed above Bluff Lake, which was situated directly below Cement Bluff. This bluff was cemented together from the calcium in the rock combining with carbonate to form calcite, a strong cementing agent. Massive boulders hung precariously from the overhanging north wall of Cement Bluff, attesting to the strength of the binding power of calcite. Soon we again encountered the Sisson-Callahan trail which descended 500' to Bull Lake below the PCT. This old trail, like many other old trails, was meant for stock animals so it follows lakes and meadows, unlike the modern expressway-like Pacific Crest Trail. We found the lack of pasturage very annoying.

At Bull Lake there were very few trees for us to take cover from the hot, desiccating rays of the sun. The grass was dry and short, but quite adequate. We rode around the small lake looking for a nice place to camp. We found a spot that had a little shade and a few fairly level areas and decided to camp there. A fisherman appeared from around one of the trees and told us the fishing was good. Since he was on his way out, I asked him for some hooks and weights. He gladly gave me all that he had, then he disappeared as suddenly as he had appeared. I then proceeded to try my luck at fishing this lake after I again untangled the line on the reel. With the first cast I had caught one. In the next hour I lost all my hooks again on some hideous creature lurking on the bottom of this lake. Well, I decided that I had enough fishing for one trip with a cheaply-made fishing rod and reel.

Morning brought us cool clear skies which by nine AM began to cloud over. We hit the trail just as the clouds let loose with a torrential downpour. I put on my Gore-Tex jacket while Jan and Mary displayed their Hefty collection. The heavy rain soon stopped but a light drizzle kept on. It was cold, but everything looked so clean and beautiful that it was nice riding. We had thirteen miles to go before we reached Scott Mountain Summit where we planned to stop for lunch.

We reached the summit in early afternoon, set up the tube tents and then picketed the horses. We sat in the tents eating, napping, and deciding what we were to do now with the light rain still falling around us. We had forty miles to go, through the Salmon-Trinity Alps Primitive Area, before we reached our pick-up point. We had less than 24 hours to ride that stretch, so we had to send word to the crew to pick us up at Scott Mountain Summit rather than Etna Summit. The rain had stopped by early evening and we enjoyed our last evening on the trail. The next morning we planned to ride into the primitive area for a short ride without the packs before they came to get us.

We were up early and had hit the trail by nine. It wasn't very long before we entered the primitive area. Within a half mile or so we came across such magnificent sights that we were speechless. We knew that we would have to ride this forty mile stretch next year with plenty of film. We continued on for another hour before we had to turn back. The tremendous views kept changing with every step we took. There was plenty of grass and water in this first part of the area.

This sixty mile stretch of the PCT was a lot more enjoyable than last year's. We had learned a lot more about the items we needed to bring. The scenery was much more spectacular and the grass and water much more plentiful. The rain did little to dampen our spirits. Next year we would take a week and really have a trail ride to remember.

Chapter 7

Jan and Mary had decided this year to start without me as I could not get the two extra days off to start with them. They started out from Scott Mountain Summit where we had stopped last year. I was to meet them at Etna Summit at noon, two and a half days later. This short stretch went through a small portion of the Salmon-Trinity Alps Wilderness Area. Unfortunately, their ride began in almost continuous rain which also dampened their spirits. This was the first part of September, so this rain was more than just a summer storm.

I met them at noon on their third day of riding. We started out after they had a quick bite of lunch. We were planning to ride eleven miles to Shelly Meadows where we would establish camp. We entered the Marble Mountain Wilderness shortly after hitting the trail. The scenery was magnificent. Two minutes after entering the wilderness, we discovered that Mary's horse, Rojo, had lost a shoe. The ground was rocky and we had a long way to go. We had spare shoes and the tools to put a new one on, but we decided to wait until we reached camp to do the job. Within minutes after setting out, I spotted a worn, rusty shoe sitting on a wooden post. It turned out to be usable, so Mary brought it along and that evening put it on Rojo.

Shelly Meadows was a large green meadow with plenty of water and places to camp. The grass was pretty short but there was still plenty of feed for overnight. The area looked like it had been used extensively by pack outfits during the summer, as well as in past years. We set up camp and were looking forward to barbequed hamburgers for dinner. It was difficult finding firewood close to camp. Some pieces had to be dragged or carried for ten minutes or more. It took us a while to get the fire going, but it wasn't long before we were enjoying dinner.

Jan was riding Villa, a six-year-old well-behaved, Arabian stallion. He wasn't used to being staked out in the field, so Jan had to hold his rope or tie it to something solid. Tonight she decided to tie him to a large rock that she could barely lift. Villa promptly swung the rock around at the end of its rope with his massive neck muscles until it collided with Jan's knee. She was very lucky to not have been severely injured. After that incident, Villa was tied up short to a tree. We examined our map and decided that we would try to make it to Paradise Lake some eighteen miles distant. With that accomplished, we turned in.

After leaving Shelly Meadows, we quickly climbed to the mountain's crest, opening up magnificent views that defy description. We soon began our steepest climb yet, ascending the switch backs up to a crest above Cliff Lake. We were fortunate this year not to have any snow on the trail above the lake. This would be virtually impassable to stock, unless you dug your way through the snow-field. This part of the PCT was even more spectacular than any we had seen before.

We stopped for lunch at Cold Spring about 250 yards down a faint trail which lay opposite the trail that went to Red Rock Valley. The trail had a lot of deadfall, but the meadow at the end was just right for the horses. The small trickling spring had good, clear water for our canteens. The ride to this point was an easy ride with fabulous scenery. The next part of today's ride appeared to be as good, if not better.

After lunch, the trail began to descend to Marble Valley Guard Station at the base of Marble Mountain. We quickly came to the fissured marble, so dazzling in the sunlight. We could also see many caves. This marble is a 600' thick stratum out of 10,000' of sediments. The water flows right through this porous rock forming the fissures and caves. This was fascinating!

We reached the bottom and were nearing the guard station. We hoped to get some information about a number of things at this ranger station. As we rounded the trail, several buildings came into view. We followed the trail as it approached the largest building straight ahead. There were many tents in an obvious camp set up off to our left. We got within 200 yards of the building when some madman ran out of the building and began shouting at us:

"GET THOSE HORSES OUT OF CAMP!"

"GET OUT OF HERE!"

That was rude to say the very least. Was that really a ranger? We hoped not, but even if it were not, why did the ranger allow such behavior? We were nowhere near their camp, and if we were, why did they have it so close to the trail?? We quickly left the guard station and continued on our way. We had a very long traverse of Black Mountain, another mountain made of marble, ahead of us before we reached Paradise Lake. This area also had many fissures and caverns in the massive mountain made of marble. Once again the views surrounding us were tremendous!

We arrived at Paradise Lake late in the afternoon, weary from our long ride. This beautiful little lake was in a glacial basin which knelt at the base of the magnificent King's Castle. The two large campsites were well within the 200' lake limit, so we chose to make our own camp under a few trees 200' away. Since it is also against regulations to camp in a meadow, we were still camped illegally. Other than the xxxx back at the guard station, we had not seen anyone yet this trip.

We were just falling asleep under the clear starlit night when suddenly the horses became very agitated. Something was out there. Mary thought she heard something heavier than a deer, but it did not sound like a bear. I knew that there had been sightings of Sasquatch in these mountains, but I really doubted that this was what was spooking the horses tonight. The horses continued to stare at the willows densely surrounding the lake's inlet about 200 yards away. We lay very quietly while trying to pick out some clue as to what type of creature we had out there. I soon fell asleep on the sloped meadow, while lying against a tree to keep from falling into the lake. Morning came upon us quickly with no further developments regarding our nocturnal visitor. The only tracks Mary could find were just a few large deer tracks over our hoof prints on the trail above the willow shrouded inlet. We were sure that it had not been a deer, as our horses were used to deer.

We headed out early because we had thirty miles to cover to reach Seiad Valley where we planned to spend the night. We traversed several wind-swept saddles with great views before we left the Marbles. We now began a long descent from 7000' down to 1300' at Seiad Valley. This was a different sort of ride. We were continuously following Grider Creek down the canyon all the way to the Klamath river. There was plenty of water throughout the middle stretch of trail. The trail turned into a paved road at Grider Creek Campground where we found several horse corrals surrounded by numerous well-kept campsites. We stopped here for lunch before riding the last 10 miles into Seiad Valley. The last piece of trail was long and very hot. The temperature had quickly climbed into the nineties as we approached 1300'. By the time we rode into town, it was seven PM and still 85 degrees.

The problem in town was to find a place to camp with food and water for our horses. All the land that we had seen since Grider Creek Campground and on was fenced, so we had no place to camp. As we rode by a trailer court, we stopped to talk with a few people sitting on chairs on the lawn. Two of them were the owners of the place and invited us to spend the night in the back. They also located and picked up a bale of hay for us. Then their hospitality extended to fresh cucumbers and tomatoes with vinegar to add to our dinner. The people in the general store were no less hospitable. We want to express thanks to these generous people in Seiad Valley, California.

We had gone to bed on a hot, humid summer's night. When we awoke it was overcast and a little cooler. We took our time while letting the horses eat their fill of alfalfa. The long climb we had waiting for us would, at least, be a little cooler today. We had another 1/4 mile walk down the highway to reach the trail. Immediately after we hit the trail, we began a steep climb. The sun was just now beginning to put in its appearance for the day. It began getting warmer as the sun again left its cover of clouds.

We had just passed Lower Devil's Peak trail when the clouds began sprinkling on us. Soon a light rain began to fall as we entered the cloud-covered mountain's crest. The wind was fierce as we crossed the saddle north of Lower Devil's Peak and headed toward Middle Devils Peak. The temperature rapidly fell as the storm began to increase in fury. We were wrapped as tightly as we could be, but still water got in. The wind was blowing from all directions, even from the bottom as we rode the crest. Within an hour we were all quite cold and partially wet as we rode past Upper Devils Peak. We were planning to stop at Kangaroo Springs, but the clouds were so thick around us that we could not tell where we were on the trail or how much further we had to go. None of us had yet mentioned the possibility of turning back, but soon it became obvious that a storm this late in the season may be worth thinking about. Our sleeping bags and spare clothes were wet and it was getting colder. Finally, I pulled us to a stop on some descending switch-backs and asked what they thought about turning back. It took us five long minutes to come to a consensus. We did not realize that we had already come sixteen miles. It was a long descent back to Seiad Valley.

That storm ended up dropping several feet of snow and copious amounts of rain in the next ten days. We were glad that we had enough sense to turn back in the face of such a storm. Now that we are warm and dry, it is hard to imagine how bad it really was out there on that mountain crest in that storm. We would have been very lucky to have survived.

Chapter 8

Because last year's attempt to reach I-5 from Seiad Valley on this stretch of the Pacific Crest Trail had to be aborted because of the severe storm, Jan, Mary, and I decided to try it again this year. We also decided to ride it a month earlier, this time in early August, rather than take chances of another early winter storm in September. This year we also had two additional riders join us: Linda and Brian. This was the first year we had additional people join us on our trip. We were hoping that they would enjoy this adventure as much as we would.

We arrived at Seiad Valley by ten AM. This was our first year with a pack horse and it took us a while to stow our supplies and load the packs. The most difficult part was trying to get both packs even in weight. The temperature was climbing well into the nineties by the time we hit the trail at 11:30. We had a 4300' climb to Kangaroo Springs which lay about ten miles away to complete today's trip.

That was a very strenuous ride from Seiad Valley to Upper Devil's Peak. The heat and lack of water took a staggering toll on the two dogs, Fuzzy and Ben. We had to stop several times waiting for them to recover. Our horses did a lot better, although it took a lot out of them as well. This ten mile stretch looked a lot different without all the rain and dense clouds we had to ride through last year. We could see Seiad Valley far below us, but the haze was too much to see back into the Marble Mountain Wilderness. We were within a few hundred yards from the springs when we realized that this was where we turned back last year. We had no idea we were so close to Kangaroo Springs. But with the severity of that storm, the springs would have been worthless to us anyway.

Kangaroo Springs were nothing more than three muddy little springlets surrounded by rocks and cow infested pasture. It was located on the south side of Kangaroo Mountain and so received plenty of sunlight. A summer thunderstorm was brewing when we arrived, so we quickly set up our tents. With that storm came strong, gusty winds that blew away Linda's dome tent, which wasn't staked down. We chased it down and staked it securely.

It never really rained on us that night. We started a small fire to barbeque our hamburgers, but in a short while had to put it out because of the wind. The hamburgers and chili beans sure tasted mighty good. We went to bed about dark to get ready for tomorrow's 18 mile ride to Alex Hole, where there was a Swiss chalet-styled outhouse I was looking forward to seeing.

This felt like a long ride for reasons unknown to me. By lunch I was getting tired and really felt that I had had enough. The views were magnificent but we had seen them all before. At lunch we had finally found some water for us and the horses. The pack horse, Chickadee, felt so tired that she tried to lie down with the packs still on. We knew something was wrong with her slightly elevated pulse. Was she tying up or beginning to colic? What was she trying to tell us? We had only eight more miles to go before we reached camp, so we decided to continue toward our destination. It was a long eight miles as I had to virtually pull Chickadee behind me. She seemed exhausted and very reluctant to move out. As it turned out, the pack saddle was not seated properly and the packs were a little off balance. This combination managed to severely gall her lower back. It looked awful and was very painful to her as we witnessed her increased pulse and contorted back. She was no longer able to carry the packs, so we had to think up plan "B."

Alex Hole seemed like a ledge carved out of a mountain facing to the north. It was forested with a spring and small pasture. The view was tremendous. There were several good campsites to choose from. I searched for several hours for that Swiss chalet-styled outhouse to no avail. I could not even find a level spot where it could have once been. I decided that it was just another trail mystery. The spring was very shallow, so I dug it out and made a two foot deep hole from which we could draw our water. However, the mud that I stirred up took until morning to clear up. At least we would have plenty of water for breakfast and our canteens. After our delicious enchiladas and Spanish rice, we went to bed knowing that tomorrow's ride would at least be an easier 16 miles to Wrangle Camp than today's ride was.

Sometime during the early morning hours we were awakened by Linda's horse snorting and blowing for all he was worth. There was something out there that he did not like. Was a bear getting ready to attack him? Maybe it was a mountain lion. None of the other horses seemed bothered by it, so I went back to sleep. In the morning Jan went down to the lower, inaccessible spring and found large fresh bear tracks. Was this really the foul creature that kept half the camp awake last night? Whatever it was, it did not get close enough to get veteran trail horses nervous.

Brian was riding a large, spirited, Quarter Horse mare named Lady. She seemed the logical choice to carry the pack. She hadn't been packed before, but she learned quickly. Brian weighed about 100 pounds, so he was ideal for Chickadee's sore back. We packed Lady and rode Chickadee; both did very well. I was thankful for the versatility and adaptability of the Quarter Horse.

The day's ride was beautiful, although there was little level ground or water found along the way. Shortly before noon we crossed the California/ Oregon border. After our short border celebration, we continued onward into the rain-infested forests of Oregon. We stopped at Donomore Meadows for lunch. This was a very large sloping meadow with water, cows, and several old wooden structures that were still standing. It would have made a nice place to camp, but we were headed for Wrangle Camp with its stone shelter, running water, stoves, and sink just eight miles ahead. About half way to Wrangle Camp we stopped at Sheep Camp for a break.

Sheep Camp had a good spring with water flowing generously from a pipe with a lot of steep sloping pasture all around it. It was also located right next to a busy, graveled road located 50' above the spring, the same road that went to Wrangle.

At Wrangle Camp we found an overflowing campground filled with University of Southern Oregon geology students finishing a six week field studies class. We searched for water and grass away from their camp, but none was to be found. We made camp in an old landing near the students' camp so we would at least have water close to us. There was enough grass for the horses, although it was not a pasture. I set up the solar shower and two of us had nice, cool showers. The dogs were beginning to tire from the many miles of traveling each day and we were beginning to worry about them. I had to wrap Fuzzy's pads with Vetrap for the next day's marathon of twenty miles.

We left Wrangle Camp early the next morning so we could get to our camp on I-5 at Callahan's for dinner. The ride seemed to go quickly and smoothly. We rode around the north side of Mt. Ashland just a little below the ski slopes. The trail merged with a snowmobile trail as we descended toward I-5. It wasn't long before the permanent PCT gave way to an obvious temporary or unfinished segment of trail. The trail became worse until it dropped a sheer ten feet to an old power-line dirt road. The temporary markers were still with us. The dirt road led us into someone's back yard where we lost the trail. Even on such a well-marked trail as the PCT we sometimes had to wonder about the people who laid it out. Since we were so close to the Mt. Ashland Highway, we proceeded down the road looking for signs of the trail that got lost in private property.

We rode about a mile on the road before spotting signs marking the trail. Once again on the trail we made good time. We arrived at Callahan's parking lot about five PM where we found the truck and trailer with hay, water, and more supplies. We rode about 21 miles today, so we were ready for an ice cold Coke and steak dinner. We took quick showers in the horse trailer and prepared for dinner. Just as we sat down, Jan's husband, John, and daughter, Linda, walked in and joined us. That was sure a pleasant surprise. The service was as good as the dinners. We had been looking forward to eating at Callahan's since last year; we were not disappointed. After dinner we went back outside to the parking lot where we had set up camp.

Fuzzy and Ben could hardly walk. We decided that the dogs had had enough, so we sent them home with John and Linda.

The next morning we left about nine AM so we could set up camp early and take showers. We had only a twelve mile ride past Pilot Rock to the fenced in spring where we would establish camp. The ride was hot and through many clear-cuts. We had reached Pilot Rock earlier than we thought we would. Our map showed crisscrossing dirt roads and jeep trails. We kept going wondering if we had passed the spring. After a few more hours, we finally came to the fenced-in spring. The horses could be turned loose to graze and we had tap water from the spring.

I set up the solar shower under the eves of a partially collapsed log cabin. It hung almost directly overhead, allowing the water to fall almost above my head. It felt invigorating. I walked back to camp, about 100 yards uphill, and sat down on a log still breathing heavily from the climb. Jan was preparing a level spot for her bedroll when she began screaming. After a minute or so, we realized she had disturbed a large timber rattlesnake. It was over five feet in length. I had never seen one so big, outside a zoo. After finishing off that killer, we searched and beat the brush around camp looking for its mate, to no avail.

With that excitement over, we began setting up our tents and preparing dinner. Dinner was wolfed down by all and we were waiting for the cherry cheesecake to jell when an extremely strong wind came up out of nowhere, leveling our camp. It blew away Linda's tent. We did not find it until the next day about ten miles away. My tent was staked, but the wind began uprooting the stakes. Then the heavy rain began. I helped Mary and Brian rig up their tube tents strung between two trees. We were all scrambling for rain gear and anchoring our tents. Soon the wind slowed down, but the rain continued on.

Later that evening I put on my Gore-Tex jacket and hood and went outside to explore the rain-soaked woods. It was a real pleasant experience walking in this warm Oregon summer rain. It was just about over as I returned to camp a few hours later. Everyone was out and about when I walked back into camp. I sure surprised them as they thought that I was still in my tent sleeping. We discussed the next day's ride which was to be an easy ten miles to Little Hyatt Reservoir. It was just about dark, so with the chores done we went to bed.

We got up again by 6:30 AM and were on the trail by nine. Today was to be a shorter ride for us. Little Hyatt Reservoir was about a mile from Hyatt Lake where there was a resort and restaurant. I was looking forward to an ice-cold Coke. The ride was uneventful for the most part. As we arrived below the waterfall formed by the dam below Little Hyatt, we came across a lovely young woman sunbathing in the nude next to the creek below the waterfall. She added a spark of interest to the otherwise dull scenery we had seen that day.

We crossed the creek and came to a dirt road leading up and around the cascading falls over the dam. On the far side of the lake, we found several nice places to establish camp. Immediately after camp was set up, I took off for the restaurant and store for my Coke. It was a short ride at Hassani's run. Soon everyone had joined me. There is something about a soft drink or beer that cuts trail dust like nothing else. That was sure refreshing.

When I returned to camp, my solar shower had heated the water almost too hot to shower with. I suffered through it.

I diluted it with cold water and it was heated sufficiently by the time the others returned. Since we had all eaten at the resort, there was no reason to cook dinner. We looked over the map and decided that our next stop would be at Howard Prairie Lake, which would be another short ten mile ride.

Our day began as usual searching for water near the trail for the horses. This whole segment of PCT from I-5 had been a difficult one for finding water. Our book described a water faucet installed for PCT hikers near Howard Prairie Lake, so we knew we would at least have water for our canteens. We came across the sign pointing the way to the faucet, which was at the end of a quarter mile long spur trail. To our astonishment the faucet had no water, again showing us the ineptness of the Forest Service in managing our national forests. We had to jump a fence onto private property and use the faucet found near a building.

Once back on the trail, we began looking for a place to camp for the night. We came across a sign indicating a horse camp off in this direction, so we followed it, never again to see another sign nor the horse camp. What did they do with it?? Another mystery we could not solve. We kept riding past the

"NO CAMPING"

signs littering the lake-shore, looking for some trace of grass until we finally found some. We were prepared to establish camp when we noticed the sign:

"NO OVERNIGHT CAMPING."

Did that mean we could camp here for the day only? We packed up again, getting more irritated as time went on. We finally found a place to camp below the dam in a cow infested pasture next to a foul-smelling canal.

There was little level ground and everywhere there were cow-pies waiting to be stepped on. With all the open spaces and countryside, we felt that the Forest Service could have done better in either routing the trail or placing realistic signs where we could camp. This, however, is beyond their ability, it seems. This was not the last of their poor management of our national resources we were to see on this stretch of trail.

After setting up camp in this depressing setting, we took another serious look at our map. We had a total of 21 miles left to go before we reached our trail's end at Highway 140. That would bring us in a day early. Halfway to the end there was a meadow on the map alongside Dead Indian Road, but the way our luck was running we did not know if we would find water and, if we did, if it would be infested with bovines as well. We decided to ride to the road junction and decide there what our course of action would be. At worst we would reach the Cascade Canal or Fish Lake at the end, so we were sure of finding water and grass.

As we rounded Old Baldy, we junctioned with the old, now defunct, Oregon Skyline trail. We could not tell which direction it had come from as its sign was so faint. Old Baldy had a lookout perched at its top many years ago, so we decided to ride up for a view. Old Baldy was not, so there was almost no view through the treetops. We went back down to the trail to continue the day's adventure.

This small stretch had a lot of deadfall for us to negotiate, but we soon came to a trail maintenance party of two clearing the trail. Past them the trail was again in good repair. We soon came to Dead Indian Road, which was a super highway of gravel, definitely not to our horses' liking. At this point we decided to ride the additional eleven miles to Fish Lake for the evening. The other motivating factor was that there was a resort there and they would have ice-cold Cokes waiting for us.

We were to complete our 21 mile trip for the day in anticipation of a nice pleasant camp near the lake. We had no idea that the Forest Service in its usual manner was to again foul us up. The last stretch of this dry, boring segment of PCT was across many miles of lava flow. It would have been impassable except for the cinder trail that was laid out across it. What slowed us down on these cinders was the addition of smaller cinders which was like riding on a rough graveled road. It was quite an accomplishment crossing this natural barrier, although it was slow going.

We were within a half mile of the highway when we saw a sign pointing one way to Fish Lake and in the other direction to the highway and the continuation of the PCT. We rode to the lake, which was an additional three miles, but we were almost there. As we neared the lake we came to another sign saying

"HORSE TRAIL."

Being the conscientious horsemen that we were, we took the horse trail which lead us to a rocky part of the lake and then dead-ended. OK, now where were we to go?? We backtracked to a dirt road and followed it around the lake to the resort, where we were met by a Forest Service official who then told us that horses are not allowed near recreational lakes here in Oregon. We had to leave the area, according to him. After some talking, he unofficially told us of a place below the lake where we would be permitted to camp. The resort owner approached us at this time and he was obviously displeased to have our party "messing up" his concession near the lake. We explained our long ride and told them we wanted to use the phone and buy some supplies. The owner's attitude quickly changed. Of course we could stay and spend our money, but then get out. On his own, the Forest Service official offered to show me the way to a real campsite below the lake that he knew about.

It was about 3.5 miles away along the busy highway to this place. When we reached it, this ideal spot had been nearly destroyed by a clear cut logging operation that was still in progress. It was, however, near the river and there was plenty of grass for our horses, though scarred by the ongoing logging operation. He was as disappointed as I was as he returned me to the resort where the others were waiting for me. I still have not figured out how they can restrict us from the lake without providing us with an alternative. Does the Forest Service take money on the side from special interest groups?

After tanking up with Cokes, we rode the additional miles to our raped campsite. This gave us a total of 26 miles for the day, and it felt like it. This camp proved to be much nicer than it looked at first sight. It did have many level spots for us to pitch our tents and there were no cow-pies - faar out! Tomorrow we had a short six mile ride back to our pick-up point, which we were all looking forward to.

The next morning we headed back through the resort, then back to where we had left the PCT. The PCT quickly came to the highway, which we crossed to the Cascade Canal on the other side. Unfortunately, we could not water the horses as the canal had no water. Oh well, we were getting used to this. We had at most a half mile more to the horse staging area where there must be water. There was not. Jan's husband was to meet us in this large PCT staging area at noon to pick us up and he would have water with him, so it was no real problem this time. We were sure glad we turned to Fish Lake for water, rather than continue on the PCT to the Cascade Canal.

Knowing about the Forest Service inefficiencies, Jan decided that she should walk her horse to the highway to wait for John. It was a good thing she did, because there turned out not to be any signs indicating that this was the PCT parking area. We again managed to outwit the Forest Service, which appears to go out of its way occasionally to make life difficult on this stretch of the PCT.

This section was the least scenic and driest section I had yet to observe. It abounded with past and present logging scars which we often passed through. If this were not enough to detract from this section's appeal, the lack of wilderness sensation and the abundance of government regulations will. This section should be avoided by all, unless someone enjoys all this or just has to hike it out of some demented form of humor. We decided that next year we would take a shorter trip and do a lot more research into our trail's water and grass situation before we hit the trail.

Chapter 9

Our hunting trip in September was exciting; no deer, but still exciting. We left the Friday, the day before deer season. Shortly after leaving town, we found the road blocked by a logging truck that had overturned and caught fire. Three hours later we decided to take a little known and little used back road to the wilderness area.

We were told to meet two people on Granite Peak, so we kept looking for the Forest Service road that went there. Finally we found the sign "Stonewall Pass Trailhead 7 miles -> ." Our map showed this as the only road in. We arrived a few hours before dark as usual. Our friends were not there; no one was there. We saddled up and were off in a flash. I was riding Kharim, Merle was on Whiskey, Ron was on Hassani, Champ was carrying a full pack, and Abby was packing for her first time.

The first hour went fine. We climbed from 3200' to about 4800'. Then the trail started running through a lot of deadfall. Abby began balking at some of the crossings and detours. I had her on a lead rope and she began stopping and no amount of pulling would budge her. Merle had to ride up behind her and give her a whack on the butt. Champ was perfect. He just followed and stayed on the trail 100' behind all of us, until we came to a steep, rugged detour. We got around the downed trees blocking the trail, but Champ was still on the other side and upset that we left him. Merle went to get him on foot, but Champ decided to go back to the trailer directly without following the trail. CRASH! BANG! CRASH! Down the tree studded slope he went with Merle hot on his trail. Ron was laughing hysterically. Twenty minutes later they were back with only a few scrapes and bruises.

It was getting dark as the trail went through some thick brush. The trail was cutting across a 40 degree slope at the time. In the middle of the brush we fell into a creek. We came out in a long, narrow, sloping meadow which we quickly crossed and then lost the trail completely in the near darkness that pervaded the forest.

We set up a crude camp on the steeply sloped meadow at 5200' overlooking Trinity Lake. We had to lay our sleeping bags on the up slope side of large boulders to keep from rolling down the mountain side. We wondered about the whereabouts of the two guys were we were to meet. Maybe they didn't make it or were still waiting for the highway to be reopened after the accident. We had a quick dinner and curled up to our favorite boulder and went to sleep. Throughout the night we were awakened by deer walking though camp one even stepped on by me.

The next morning after a good hearty breakfast, we hunted deer while searching for the trail that eluded us in the dark last night. We didn't see a deer but we did find our trail. It had branched in the middle of the brush were we fell into the creek. We saddled up and were off. Within a hundred yards along the creek, Abby lost her footing and plunged three feet to the bottom of the creek. Now she would not budge. Only after repeated whacks on her butt, and gentle coaxing and prodding did she finally consent to follow us. This was repeated many times in the next six grueling hours.

As the top of the mountain began to appear to be within reach, Kharim caught his left rear leg on an old smooth piece of telephone wire. He freaked! He began rearing, jumping. My left boot got stuck in the left stirrup as Abby raced around us down slope, then up in front of us and pulling the lead rope tight around my right foot and stirrup. This was now a frightening situation. Kharim was still dancing and rearing. Merle came to our rescue. It took five minute to get untangled and straightened out. Now Abby was in front of us and wouldn't move!

We finally reached the top. We were now at 6800'. The view was magnificent so we stopped for 45 minutes for lunch. We then began to wonder where the next meadow was. We expected to find one here, but it was all rock. The trail was easy to see and follow on the map so we set out in search of our meadow.

The trail was still climbing and even Kharim was showing signs of being tired. The trail began switch-backs on a very steep, loose, decomposed granite slope. Several times the tread was so faint and covered by game trails that we lost it. I was in the lead pulling Abby when I could no longer find the trail. Merle would backtrack until he found it. I would then attempt to turn Kharim only to find Abby in front of us, once more refusing to move. This happened a dozen or more times. It was tiring and frustrating.

We finally reached a flat point where we stopped for a break and got our bearings. The slope was a good 60 degrees on the last 1/4 mile of trail. It had traversed and climbed across the face of Granite Peak at about 8000'. We did not want to return this way, but we did not know of an alternate route.

We continued on to find the trail literally dropping off the mountain again on loose decomposed granite. The trail was very steep and twice we lost the packs on Abby as they slipped off. Fortunately she did not panic or move. When the packs were again cinched up and we ready to ride again, Abby would not move. We also lost the trail several times as we did on the previous stretch. Abby would again be in front of me and would not move after we turned around to get back on our lost trail. All of this was taking place on this 60 degree slope with very loose footing.

We finally reached the cover of forest and the trail began to be more level as we continued to descend the mountain. Where were our friends? It was nearing dark again and still they were not to be found. We reached the bottom of the canyon and ran into a hunter. We inquired as to the whereabouts of Red Mountain Meadows.

He looked startled when he saw us, but pointed down the trail and said that it was about a half mile. He then asked, " You didn't come off Granite Peak, did you?"

"Yes," I replied.

"That trail has been closed to horses for years because it was too dangerous. The forest service doesn't even maintain it any more," he stated excitedly.

We continued on knowing for sure we didn't want to go back that way. A little while later we still hadn't found the meadow when we ran into another hunter. He gave us directions back the way we came. He was also surprised that we attempted, much less succeeded, in traversing Granite Peak.

We soon came to a small, dry meadow with one tree close to the edge. We set up camp and began a fire to cook our sirloin tip roast that had been soaking in teriyaki marinade for two days. I prepared our cherry cheesecake for dessert as the meat cooked. Merle was removing the meat from the grill and dropped it into the coals. After rinsing it off he put it back on the fire to warm it up.

Out of the dark walked John, one of the friends we were to meet yesterday. He was just in time for dinner. We asked where he came from. He pointed "down there." He said it was only an easy one hour walk from the trailhead.

"What trailhead? It took us ten hours on a treacherous trail!" I exclaimed wildly.

"The Stonewall Pass Trailhead. It's only three miles from here," John said.

We then told him of our ordeal over Granite Peak. He said that trail was closed when the new Stonewall Pass was built, but they haven't changed the road signs or the Trinity Alps Wilderness maps yet. He found it hard to believe we took that trail. He then told us he and the Indian would see us in the morning.

The temperature throughout the night remained in the high sixties, which was unusual for 7100' in mid-September. It was a quiet, warm, moonlit night. We slept well until we were rudely awakened by some unknown noise, After several minutes we saw in the meadow a lone doe. We got up just before dawn and got a big fire going even though it was already 70 degrees out. We waited for John. And waited......

By ten we decided to eat without him. Merle then went hunting, while Ron and I set up our chairs overlooking the arid meadow. If a buck wanted to get close enough, we were ready. It was a beautiful, sunny day. We didn't even see a rabbit.

Merle came back and he said it was eerie. He didn't see any animals. We lounged around all afternoon wondering what happened to John.

At one point a pack string came through and talked to us a while. They were surprised that we took the old Granite Peak trail. They had been on it 20 years before when it was still well maintained. Even then it was dangerous. They related a story of a veterinarian who turned his horse into the mountain and fell to his death. They said we were very lucky no one was hurt.

By five we had not heard from John, so we saddled up and headed down the trail shouting and looking for him. After riding for nearly half an hour, we decided to head back. It was a long steep ascent, but with no pack horses and the saddle stock rested up we made it back up to our camp in minutes. We were hungry!

Ron got the fire going. While I prepared the meat and fixings for the fajitas, Merle went out hunting again. The freeze-dried raspberry cobbler was a snap to prepare.

An hour before dark Merle came back saying he still did not see anything. We ate dinner and were about to start dessert, when out of the shadows stepped John and Bob. Just in time for dessert. We asked what happened to him this morning. He said they both went hunting all day, but saw nothing.

"Deer are low," said Bob.

All the experienced hunters said deer were high. High on what? The Indian said low. We decided to pack up tomorrow and head for Silago Meadows at 8000'. No one listened to Bob.

We were ready to go by 9 AM. The first stretch over Stonewall Pass was an easy ride. The fantastic views of the Trinity Alps and Trinity Lake were indescribable. The horses were all doing great until we neared Van Matre Meadows, when several of them began to act up. Ron could not get Hassani to go any further. Hassani reared and then fell over. Ron jumped just before Hassani would have fallen on him. Hassani took off back up the trail to the pass. Merle began chasing Hassani. I was on the ground trying to calm the other horses and Ron when a hundred yards up the trail a large bear thundered out of the brush running away from us. We spent a half hour fixing the packs and calming down. For the next half mile Merle walked point with his 30-06 at the ready.

We soon came to a trail junction and a worn Forest Service sign. The sign pointed to a narrow trail that said Stonewall Pass. We just came from Stonewall Pass. Ron then found a very old rusted sign that appeared to have punched in it

"Little Sto   ss."

We figured that this meant Little Stonewall Pass, so we started up this narrow trail.

The initial steep ascent began to level out as the trail widened into a large conifer forest. Now the deadfall began forcing more detours upon us. We had very little trouble here. Abby was learning the ropes and didn't balk as often. As we neared the top, our trail left the forest and became even steeper and more narrow than before. We reached the top of the pass without any incidents before noon. We decided to take a break and let everyone rest.

We left the pass at shortly after noon. We guessed that the large meadow below us was Silago. It looked like an easy ride to the bottom. The trail was very steep going down. Ron got off and walked for awhile until Hassani stepped on his heel. After the right amount of cussing, Ron climbed back into the saddle. We came to another trail junction. This one was on our map. To continue on to the meadow, the sign said to take the right fork. Our map showed both going to the meadow. By now we realized that we hadn't passed the lake on our right like we were expecting to. The map must be wrong.

Soon our right fork began a moderate ascent. The forest became more dense, but the trail was clear of deadfall. We continued on. Abby began to balk more and more. She was getting tired. By two-thirty the trail began to climb steeply as we left the cover of the forest. We could soon see our meadow way below us. The top was only a little way ahead, so we pushed on.

We reached the top to find a sign stating simply:

"Stock Animals Not Permitted Hazardous Trail"

There was also a sign that said Granite Lake Trail. How had we gotten here? Did we miss a trail somewhere? It was getting late and we were getting tired. The lake was a mile and a half away. We pushed on. The trail was steep, but easier and less hazardous than many others we had been on this trip. We reached Gibson Meadow a half mile below the lake just about dark.

Exhausted, we decided to have a quick easy dinner of steak and chili beans. The temperature began to drop. Our eve-

nings had been in the mid sixties until now. It had dropped into the low fifties tonight.

After dinner a pack string of about 25 horses came through, presumably to the lake above. They came back through just after midnight. We were up early and found that we had several other horse camps in our meadow. We were cleaning up our dishes when we heard a thundering sound. Ron was first to see the stampede heading our way. A dozen or more horses came charging through our camp. All our horses were tied, except Champ. He did not want to leave Abby, so he stayed. Kharim got tangled in the rope and gashed his front leg, a bad wound. After applying a dressing, were ready to go.

Several guys came through our camp chasing after their wayward horses. We found out that in Mumford Basin there were bears. These hunters lost a tent and an ice chest. Well, we had decided earlier that was where we were headed. No bears were going to disturb us. No siree, Bob! We headed out merrily on our way. We met the Twin Lakes Trail in less than an hour. The trail to Mum-ford was two miles ahead. We were told that at the junction, take the left fork then the right fork. OK. This was another cakewalk through a forest with plenty of creek crossings and level areas. We soon came to our first junction and turned left. We came to a narrow bridge with low rope sides. Kharim was not going to cross it! Whiskey, Merle, and Champ crossed without a problem. Ron tried to walk Hassani across, but that wasn't working either. Kharim got tired of waiting so he crossed. Surprisingly, Abby followed. Ron walked down to the creek and there amidst a lot of cussing.

About twenty minutes later we remembered that we had forgotten about the fork in the trail. Ron said it was back past the bridge and it was a very faint tread to the left. I remembered seeing that, but thought it just went to a campsite by the creek. We pushed on. The cabin and meadow were at most three miles ahead. Before we realized it, we were at the edge of the meadow. It was getting dark so we thought we had missed the cabin. We found a very nice cow camp and quickly set up camp. It was getting cold and dark. The thermometer was reading 28 degrees and it was about ten PM.

Suddenly we heard a noise in the meadow where Kharim was tied. The other were loose, grazing. Then we heard the thunder of hoofbeats. We raced out from around the large brush we were camped behind. In the blackness we could see nothing. I found the spot where Kharim had been tied. No Kharim. He had broken the 3/4 inch cotton rope. What had spooked them? We were hoping it was not another bear. We began searching, knowing that we could very well get lost out here in the dark. We were at 7700' and the temperature was now 25 degrees. Even with our three flashlights, the trail was nearly impossible to see. We spread out, trying to keep each other in sight. We could hear the horses ahead, but it took quite a while longer to catch them. Whiskey was already hobbled, which slowed their escape.

Now the question became: Where was the camp? We hadn't had time to start a fire, nor light the lantern. The cold was cutting through our warm clothing. Ron and I held the horses while Merle scouted somewhere for the meadow and our camp. After numerous false starts, we finally made it back to camp about one AM. Kharim had again injured his bad leg. It was more swollen. I redressed it and hoped the cold night would keep the inflammation down. We would stay here a few days to rest up and plan the continuation of our journey.

We spent the next day just basking in the spectacular beauty of it all. We began searching for the cabin that was shown on the map. Merle hunted early morning and again in the late afternoon. I rode Whiskey all the way back to the bridge and back. There was no trace of it. I rode on up to the end of the basin and there was no evidence a cabin ever existed here. The highs were in the forties, but it was sunny and somewhat warm in the sun. Hassani was looking better by afternoon, and it was decided to head out of Mumford Basin and make it back to Silago Meadows. We were getting low on Cokes, but we had plenty of food. We prepared dinner keeping a watchful eye out for bears.

The following morning was overcast and very cold. A slight wind was blowing down the canyon from the glacier above. We waited until the horses were full, then we saddled up. We all looked for the cabin, but never saw it. We approached the end of the basin and I kept telling Ron to look for the fork in the trail to the right. Abby was doing fine while I kept examining the map. There was a faint tread heading off to the left. We continued on to the was a small doe drinking from our lake. We quickly got up and built a fire. Fortunately we had kept some wood covered to keep it dry. There was not a cloud in the sky. Other than the snow, there was little evidence that there had been a storm last night. We ate the last of the sausages and eggs for breakfast. Merle then went out hunting while Ron and I prepared to pack up.

We were back on the trail by noon. We came down from the basin to a creek crossing at Deer Creek Camp. Here we met the Deer Creek Trail. Heading south, it would take us to Silago Meadows where were trying to go to several days ago. Ater several miles of following the creek up the canyon, we came into a wide snow-covered meadow surrounded by magnificent peaks, one of which we had climbed as we skirted the meadow the other day.

While we were arguing about which way the trail might go, a young volunteer ranger on horseback appeared. She was more than happy to lead us for a way, but said that the trail was too hazardous for horses and that she would go the other way. We had already been on that part of the trail and it was a very strenuous climb to the top. Abby kept trying to slow us down by balking several times. There was little snow on the trail to impede us. It was all downhill from here. We would bypass dry Van Matre Meadows and continue on to Red Mountain Meadows where we had left John and Bob.. It was a race to the bottom, but the trail began once again to climb. Although the climb back up to Stonewall Pass was very steep, it was short and Abby didn't balk once. She must have recognized that this was the way home.

We soon arrived at our old campsite next to the small, dry meadow. We set up camp and built a large fire. We had one large meal left, and plenty of smaller, less appetizing ones. We debated how we were going to go back. None of us wanted to go back over Granite Peak. The other way out to the new trailhead was 17 miles to our truck, with 6 miles along Highway 3. We began cooking the elk stew and pondered the problem. Merle then told us that he had to be back by two PM tomorrow. Now, either way we had to race like the wind for home.

We were about ready to eat when we noticed the horses were intensely interested in something out there. It took us a minute but we soon saw the two hunters coming down the trail. It was John and Bob in time for dinner again. While enjoying this meal we continued discussing our dilemma. Which way to go??

"I'll drive you all to you all's truck," piped in John.

"I can't believe this! We will get to bypass that killer trail."

"Are you sure? Are you leaving tomorrow AM?"

OK, it was all set. John gave Merle his watch so we could meet him at ten at their camp. Then Merle hunted with them as they went back to their camp. He was so warm from the hike that he left his jacket at their camp... along with the watch.

We were packed up and ready to go early. We guessed it was about ten. We were off. It took less than ten minute to get to their camp, only to find there was no camp there any more. OK, they must be waiting for us down the trail. Ten minutes later we found a note attached to a stick stuck in the ground.

It read:

Phil and Murl see you at the pipe with Water

A little cryptic, but we got the message. We were riding fast but we still couldn't catch them. Soon we came to a culvert with water passing under the trail. We knew we were out of the wilderness. Scratched into the trail with a stick was another message from them. Before we knew it, we were at the new Stonewall Pass Trail-head that wasn't shown on the map. It is posted correctly from the highway, but we had come from the north and ran into the old sign first which hadn't been taken down. We didn't get Merle home by two but we had fun trying.

www.ingramcontent.com/pod-product-compliance
Lightning Source LLC
Chambersburg PA
CBHW031409040426
42444CB00005B/478